THE MARCH OF WILLIAM OF ORANGE THROUGH DEVON

and his voyage from the Netherlands

Philip Badcott

Copyright © 2022 Philip Badcott
All rights reserved
Cover photo © Philip Badcott
Map by Philip Badcott

No part of this book may be reproduced in any form or by written, electronic or mechanical, including photocopying, recording, or by any information retrieval system without written permission of the author.

Published by the author.

Although every precaution has been taken in the preparation of this book, the publisher and author assume no responsibility for errors or omissions. Neither is any liability assumed for damages resulting from the use of information contained herein.

FORWARD

I've always been fascinated by the statue of William of Orange standing on the harbourside at Brixham in South Devon, but for years I knew little about him. As a boy someone told me that he landed in 1688 on the outskirts of Brixham at Fishcombe Cove in a single ship, accompanied by a small contingent of soldiers and somehow made it to London. But that version of accounts did not ring true with me and I decided to make my own study of the man that became William III.

I discovered that the story of the invasion of William of Orange in 1688 is astonishing and its outcome changed the course of English history. He and his 15,000 soldiers sailed from the Netherlands, down the English Channel and daringly landed in Brixham in South Devon on a cold November day from where he commenced his march to London and was crowned king in April 1689.

The story of William of Orange has understandably filled many books and this volume puts the spotlight on what he did, where he went and who he met in the county he first marched through. The book also explains the build up to his decision to come to England, his preparations and his voyage.

Like many authors of the story of William of Orange, I have drawn on the diaries of those who accompanied William on his journey from the Netherlands to London as well as other accounts of the time. However, several accounts of his journey use the term 'Holland' which was in the time of William of Orange the term loosely used for 'The United Provinces' now known as the Netherlands. I have throughout (except when quoting text) used the term 'the Netherlands'.

Using these accounts and my knowledge of my county of Devon, I have pieced together his complete march from his arrival in Brixham to Axminster before he crossed the county border into Somerset and beyond. It remains a fascinating story.

Philip Badcott (June 2022)

ACKNOWLEDGEMENTS

My sincere thanks are extended to those who have helped and encouraged me in producing this short history of the march of William of Orange through Devon. These include the staff at Brixham Heritage Museum who a few years ago gave me access to its archives, the Torquay Museum Society whose library holds early copies of books, letters and maps and the Devon Heritage Centre that holds other relevant and little known documents. All three archives provided a wealth of information.

My thanks are also extended to Rowena Coote and Alan Henshaw for carefully reading my drafts and suggesting amendments. Those mentioned and others have supported me in my endeavours. Images that are not attributed are from the author's collection.

This book is dedicated to my friend Alan Henshaw. After I had researched the journey of William of Orange as far as Newton Abbot, it was he who encouraged and inspired me to complete the story of 'The March of William of Orange through Devon'.

ABOUT THE AUTHOR

Philip Badcott is a Devonian and was born in Torquay and has lived in the town for most of his life. Educated at Homelands Technical High School in Torquay and the College of St Mark and St John in Plymouth, he enjoyed a varied career working for the telecommunications company BT, Devon County Council and running his own leadership and management training company. He now studies the history of Devon and its people and has presented dozens of talks to clubs and societies. This is his third book, the others being 'History Tours of Torquay' and 'The Boatmen of Babbacombe Bay' which were published in 2021.

CONTENTS

	Page
1. Introduction	1
2. Why did William of Orange come to England?	4
3. Some research sources	11
4. The preparations for the journey from the Netherlands	13
5. The voyage from the Netherlands to England	16
6. The landing at Brixham	20
7. The march from Brixham to Exeter	29
8. William of Orange in Exeter	43
9. From Exeter to Honiton and Axminster	51
10. The march into Somerset and on to London	58
11. The legacy of William of Orange in Devon	60
12. References	62
13. Index	64

LIST OF ILLUSTRATIONS

Page

Front cover   The William of Orange statue at Brixham

Frontispiece   William III

Figure 1	Map of South and East Devon	2
Figure 2	The genealogy of William of Orange III	3
Figure 3	The William of Orange statue inscription	5
Figure 4	The mouth of the River Dart	13
Figure 5	The high cliffs between Torbay and the River Dart	20
Figure 6	Brixham Harbour at low tide	23
Figure 7	The first Brixham monument to William of Orange	27
Figure 8	Fleet Mill Lane in South Devon	30
Figure 9	Parliament House, Longcombe	32
Figure 10	The base of the old cross in Newton Abbot	36
Figure 11	Forde House in Newton Abbot	38
Figure 12	William of Orange entering Exeter	42
Figure 13	Stepcote Hill, Exeter	43
Figure 14	The Bishop's Throne in Exeter Cathedral	43
Figure 15	The ruins of the medieval Exe Bridge	44
Figure 16	Map of Exeter circa 1616	44
Figure 17	The Old Deanery in Exeter	47
Figure 18	Exeter Cathedral in the 18th century	47
Figure 19	The site of the Dolphin Inn at Honiton	52
Figure 20	The commemoration plaque at Honiton	52
Figure 21	Loughwood Meeting House	55
Figure 22	The old Roman road south of the A35 trunk road	55
Figure 23	The River Axe and its flood plain near Axminster	56
Figure 24	William III Royal Coat of Arms	59
Figure 25	The Westgate plaque in Exeter	61

William of Orange III afterwards William III

CHAPTER 1

INTRODUCTION

Brixham is a fishing and tourist town in South Devon and sits on the southern tip of Torbay. Many visitors to Brixham are familiar with the statue of William of Orange by the harbourside. It's often surrounded by tourists who use its base as a seat to enjoy their lunchtime fish and chips, or to take in the charm of Torbay's smallest town. However, many are probably completely unaware that the man commemorated on the statue came to England in 1688 to lead an invasion that would change the course of British history.

It was on 5 November that year that William Prince of Orange, also known as William of Orange III, first set foot on English soil in the fishing port of Brixham in South Devon. Amazingly, he was accompanied by nearly 15,000 soldiers and 3,000 horses, all brought to England by a fleet of nearly 500 ships.

Crowds lined the cliffs of the bay to watch his arrival, and what an amazing sight that must have been on that cold and misty November day to witness so many ships entering Torbay. It was either a welcoming sight or a terrifying sight, depending upon one's allegiance or not to King James II and one's religious persuasion – Protestant or Roman Catholic.

Shortly after William of Orange stepped onto dry land at the old pier at Brixham Harbour, he commenced his march to London to claim the throne of Great Britain and Ireland. Devon had never seen anything like it and never will.

His journey was audacious and courageous, but never reckless. It's exciting, yet pragmatic and a lesson in strategic planning, organisation and leadership.

But who was he and why did he come? Who did he meet and what did he see in Devon? These and other questions will be answered in this story of the march of William of Orange through Devon in 1688.

When I present this story as a talk to clubs and societies I'm often asked one particular question: 'Why did William of Orange choose to land at Brixham?' It's a fascinating question with an equally fascinating answer which is included in this account of William of Orange.

His march through Devon took him from Brixham to Paignton, Newton Abbot, Chudleigh and on to Exeter where William stayed for eleven days. He then marched on to Honiton, probably via Ottery St Mary and finally to Axminster before marching out of Devon and into Somerset.

The march of William of Orange through Devon in 1688

Figure 1 - Map of South and East Devon

TIMELINE OF WILLIAM OF ORANGE IN DEVON

Arrives at Brixham	5 November 1688
Marches to Paignton	6 November 1688
Marches to Newton Abbot	7 November 1688
Marches to Chudleigh and Exeter	8 & 9 November 1688
At Exeter	9 to 20 November 1688
Marches to Honiton	21 November 1688
Marches to Axminster	22 November 1688
Marches out of Devon	24 or 26 November 1688

WHO WAS WILLIAM OF ORANGE?

William of Orange was a member of the House of Orange that was originally from the medieval principality of Orange in Southern France. In 1688, he was the Head of State of the United Provinces now known as the Netherlands. He was not a monarch or a president, but the 'provincial executive officer' and held the title of Stadholder from 1672 until his death in 1702.

He was born in The Hague on 4 November 1650, but his father William of Orange II died just eight days before he was born. His mother, Mary Henrietta, was the eldest daughter of Charles I, the beheaded monarch. Thus William of Orange was a grandson of the beheaded English king.

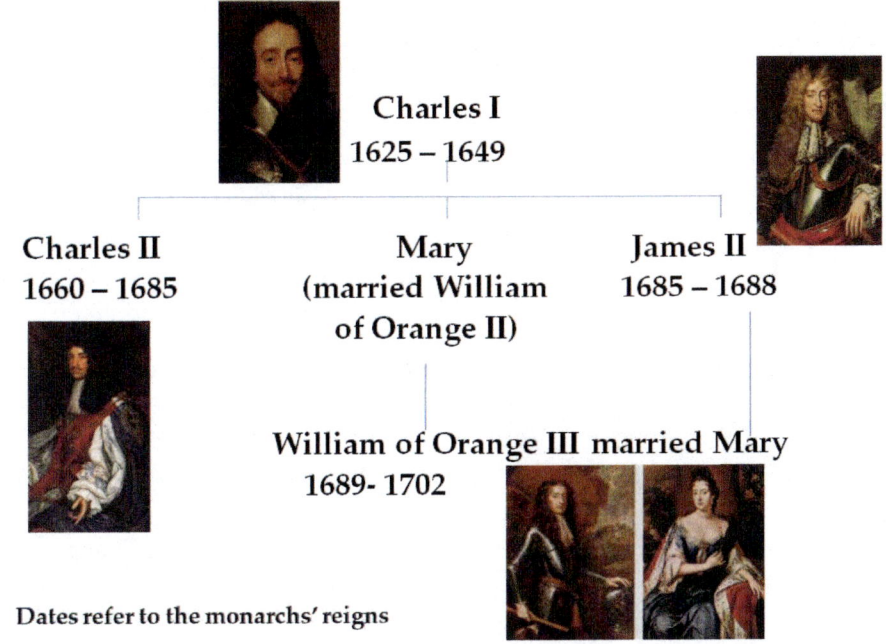

Dates refer to the monarchs' reigns

Figure 2 – the genealogy of William of Orange III

On 4 November 1677, William married his cousin Mary on his 27th birthday. She was the eldest daughter of King James II, the son of Charles I. So Mary, like her husband William, was also a grandchild of Charles I. The scene was already being pieced together for William and Mary to make a claim on the British throne because they were both members of the House of Stuart.

It is said that whilst William of Orange looked calm to the outside world, he had a shocking temper and was an awfully fiery man often lecturing others. Another account describes him as cold and calculating. However, he was a man of principle and dedicated much of his life to protecting the freedom of the Protestant religion and banishing the power of the Roman Catholics in his own country and subsequently in England.

CHAPTER 2

WHY DID WILLIAM OF ORANGE COME TO ENGLAND?

At Brixham Harbour there are two memorials to commemorate the arrival of William of Orange. The largest and most recent one - the one on the cover of this book and mentioned in the introduction – had its foundation stone laid on 5 November 1888 to celebrate the bicentenary of William's landing. It has an inscription that gives a clue about why he came. It says this:

'William Prince of Orange, afterwards William III, King of Great Britain and Ireland, landed near this spot 5th November 1688 and issued his famous declaration:

The Liberties of England and the Protestant Religion,
I WILL MAINTAIN'

There is no doubt that William of Orange sailed from the Netherlands to England to maintain both its liberties and its protestant religion. Since 1685, England had had a Roman Catholic monarch, King James II and he was the first Roman Catholic monarch since Queen Mary I (also known as Mary Tudor) who reigned from 1553 to 1558. When James II came to the throne it brought fears and worries that the country would revert from the Protestant religion and back to Roman Catholicism. William of Orange was the man who was asked to come and save the country.

The statue is of grey Sicilian marble and depicts William of Orange addressing the crowd who witnessed his landing. He has his right foot on a stone, representing his first step onto English soil. His right hand is holding his plumed hat and his left hand is on his heart, symbolising his religious beliefs and dedication to his task of maintaining the Protestant religion.

The 17th century had been extremely turbulent. It had seen the English Civil War, the beheading of Charles I, the years of the Commonwealth ruled by the Puritan Oliver Cromwell, the restoration of the monarchy and the crowning of Charles II. Then there was the Plague, the Great Fire of London and the ongoing suspicions that the monarchs wanted to revive the cause of the Roman Catholics and the fear of persecution.

Although Charles I, who reigned from 1625 to 1649, was a Protestant, he had favoured a High Anglican form of worship that made his subjects suspicious that he had Roman Catholic tendencies. He had also recruited Roman Catholics to fight for him in the Civil War and he eventually paid with his life after being found guilty of treason. His son, Charles II, who reigned from 1660 to 1685 was a secret Roman Catholic and officially converted to Catholicism on his deathbed. Then, despite the efforts of the leading Protestants in the land, James, Duke of York, became James II on the death of his brother and he was a Roman Catholic.

Figure 3 – the William of Orange statue inscription

Concerns had arisen as early as 1671 when James, then the Duke of York, startled the nation by announcing that he had converted to the Roman Catholic faith. Immediately there were worries about the succession to the crown. England just could not have a Roman Catholic monarch who would automatically become the head of the Protestant Church of England. MPs were petitioned by constituents and urged to do what they can to ensure that James reverted to being a Protestant. But to no avail.

There was also concern that James was to marry Mary of Modena who too was a Roman Catholic and any offspring would also share its parents' religion and eventually be a second Roman Catholic monarch.

It is difficult, and maybe impossible, for a 21st-century mind to be in the mindset of a 16th-century Protestant who found having a Roman Catholic monarch absolutely abhorrent. In the 21st century we seek harmony between the different religions and, by and large achieve this. In the 17th century it was the fear of persecution and the huge differences in religious belief that were causing concern. For example, the Roman Catholic Church believes in transubstantiation, where, at the Eucharistic (also known as Holy Communion) the bread and wine turns into the body and blood of Christ, whilst the Church of England opposes and rejects this belief.

The reasons why a Roman Catholic must not be the monarch go back to the reign of Henry VIII. By 1537, the Church in England had separated from the Roman Catholic Church and the authority of the Pope, to become the Protestant Church of England, with Henry VIII, now a Protestant as head of the Church. All future monarchs had to be Protestants to ensure the Protestant faith was maintained. The exception was Mary Tudor, who reigned from 1553 to 1558. Her reign brought terror with, for example, the burning at the stake of religious dissidents.

So the future James II announcing in 1671 that he was a Roman Catholic, successfully revived those ancient fears about the fate of Protestants at the hands of Mary Tudor. It was the fear of burning at the stake and an agonising death.

However, in the first two years of his reign, James II tried to appease his people and thought that he could remain a Roman Catholic and be the head of the Church of England. But his frustration of not being able to have Roman Catholics in high office and positions of authority came to a head in 1687 and 1688, when there were three events that sparked the actual rebellion against him.

In November 1685 King James prorogued parliament. Then, 17 months later in April 1687, and acting on his own authority, the king suspended the laws against the Roman Catholics by issuing his 'Declaration for Liberty of Conscience'. In modern eyes it seems perfectly fair because it allowed Roman Catholics, non conformists and political and religious dissenters, as well as Protestants – in other words, everyone - full political and religious rights. However, James II saw this as his opportunity to put Roman Catholics into positions of authority. For example, he had a purge of army officers and replaced them with Roman Catholics, and he forced the election of Roman Catholics to controlling positions in the universities of Oxford and Cambridge.

Many were delighted with the 'Declaration'. These included, as well as the Roman Catholics, the dissenting ministers who had from 1662 in the reign of Charles II lost their positions as clergymen in the Church of

England. They had refused to publicly declare, as required under the 1662 Act of Uniformity, their agreement to everything contained in the Book of Common Prayer and hence refused to conform to the Church of England form of worship. The penalty was imprisonment. Others in favour of the 'Declaration' were the ministers and congregations of Independent Churches who were hounded by the authorities in the reign of Charles II for worshipping contrary to the practices of the Church of England.

A group of dissenting ministers in the western part of Somerset and in Taunton even wrote to the James II sending him 'hearty thanks' for his 'declaration for liberty of conscience' that had established 'quiet, ease, peace, and welfare of all your subjects'.

One Devon rector who approved of the Declaration for Liberty of Conscience was Robert Woolcombe, the rector of Moretonhampstead. In 1662, he was forced to quit his post being unhappy with the Act of Uniformity and he and many of his flock met in secret, sometimes in the woods. In 1665 he was expelled from Moretonhampstead under the 1665 Five Mile Act. This Act of Parliament forbade ministers who refused to adhere to the Act of Uniformity to come within five miles of any place where they had been the parson. The parson was now out of reach from those who could provide practical support and was the ruin of many. Attempting to return, Robert Woolcombe was arrested and imprisoned. In February 1687, he paid for an expensive licence to allow him to continue to preach to his dissenting congregation and then, seven weeks later, gained his religious freedom when the Declaration for Liberty of Conscience was announced by James II.

The members of the Independent Church at Weycroft (known later as the Congregational Church) on the outskirts of Axminster also experienced persecution under Charles II and welcomed the 'Declaration'. The Axminster Ecclesiastica (the church records of the Independent Church in the town), records that in 1681, the worshipers were forced to leave their chapel and: 'wandered up and down, sometimes in one place, or wood, sometimes in another... and thus they continued steadfastly in their assembling together...'

A Devon example of James II putting the sinister side of his Declaration for Liberty of Conscience into action, was at Totnes in December 1687 where Sir Edward Seymour of Berry Pomeroy Castle was the Recorder. His responsibilities included being the Town Clerk, a judge and the one who selected those who would stand for Parliament. James II dismissed him from his duties and ordered the 39 Town Council members to vote in John Southcote who was a Roman Catholic. Of the 39 members, 33 voted against this order so James dismissed 17 of the 33 and replaced them with Catholics, dissidents and non conformists. Not surprisingly, at the second vote, John Southcote was appointed as the Recorder. A Roman Catholic and supporter of James II now had significant powers in Totnes. And this was happening all over England. Protestants in positions of authority were being replaced by supporters of James II.

In 1687, James II also set aside the Test Act which stipulated that all public office holders must take Holy Communion in the Church of England, and the Act therefore excluded Roman Catholics from Parliament. It was James II's opportunity to appoint Roman Catholics to high office right at the centre of government and for Roman Catholics to stand for parliament. For example, in Somerset in February 1688 many of his supporters were appointed as Deputy Lieutenants and Justices of the Peace.

Then on 2 July 1687, King James dissolved Parliament and keen to ensure support for him before another parliament was called, he asked three questions of the country's gentry and others likely to aspire to a seat in parliament. The King's aim was to coerce them gently into only suggesting members of Parliament that would be acceptable to him. The questions were:

1) Do you agree for the removal of the Test Act?
2) Will you assist and contribute to the election of such members who shall be for the removal of the Test Act?
3) Will you support the King's 'Declaration for Liberty of Conscience' by living friendly with those of all persuasions?

In Somerset for example, out of 30 who were approached, twelve answered 'Yes' in all three questions. But King James did not have it all his own way. There were two who agreed only to two questions and 16 who would only agree to question three. Who wouldn't want to live on friendly terms with everyone? Imagine these proceedings taking place across all the counties of England.

Towards the end of 1687, James II was considering repealing the Penal Laws and the Test Act and sought the opinions of his son-in-law William of Orange and daughter Princess Mary. An account of this is in a letter dated 8 January 1688 now held at the Devon Heritage Centre written to Sir William Courtenay at 'Ford near Excester, Devonshire'. The house is now known as Forde House in Newton Abbot. The letter was addressed to him as 'Dear Brother' and signed W.W. who was almost certainly William Waller, the brother-in-law of Sir William Courtenay. Waller, who had fled to the continent, knew William of Orange and had met him in The Hague. The letter informs Courtenay that William of Orange and his wife Princess Mary had:

'twice been earnestly solicited by the English Envoy at The Hague from the King that they would give their consent to the repealing of the Penal Acts and the Test Act but have been positively refused, alleging that it would be the destruction of the Protestant Religion opening thereby a door for the Papists to be admitted into all employment, military and civil.'

James II was probably disappointed and maybe alarmed at the lack of support from his daughter and son-in-law. William and Mary were, however, in favour of the Penal Laws against the Protestant Dissenters being repealed, but only through a freely elected Parliament. William Waller ends the letter asking Sir William Courtenay to let him know his own views and the views of others in Devon about the matter. The letter certainly demonstrates the intrigue in London, The Hague and Devon about the religious tension between Protestants, its Dissenters and Roman Catholics, and the tension between James II and his daughter and son-in-law.

Another example of one who refused to agree to the repeal of the Test Act was Admiral Arthur Herbert who was also Master of the Robes in King James II's household. When asked by the king if he supported the removal of the Test Act, he answered that he: 'could not do it either in honour nor conscience'. He was dismissed from his duties after which William of Orange invited him to join him in the Netherlands.

No doubt pleased with the support for question three, James issued the 'Declaration for Liberty of Conscience' for a second time on 7 April 1688 and ordered that it be read in all churches. Its aim was to convince the country that he was firm in his resolution to remain monarch and deter any plots against him. However, the growing discontent resulted in indirect overtures to William of Orange. In late April 1688, Edward Russell visited William in The Hague and pleaded with him: 'come with an army this year or don't bother. We will act without you'. Some say that William hesitated, others say he agreed but only if he received a formal invitation.

He took action when it was announced in June 1688 that the Queen had given birth to a son also called James. William's chance of succession through birth was lost with this birth of a prince. Another twist in the tale is that many believed that the baby boy was not Mary of Modena's and a new born baby had been secretly brought into her bedchamber when she was (supposed to be) in labour although there was never any conclusive evidence to prove that the baby was not her son.

For leading Protestants in the land it was all too much and in that same month of June 1688, a group of seven Protestant politicians and nobles turned to William of Orange III, a Stuart and grandson of Charles I to invade England and with his wife Mary claim the throne. The full and formal invitation was drafted by Henry Sidney, dated the 30 June 1688, and signed by what became known as 'The Immortal 7'. In place of their signatures, a two digit secret code was used for each of the seven. The letter was taken to The Hague by Arthur Herbert disguised as an ordinary sailor. This is a transcript:

'We have great satisfaction to find by 35, and since by M. Zulestein, that your Highness is so ready and willing to give us such assistances as they have related to us. We have great reason to believe that we shall be every day in a worse condition than we are and less able to defend ourselves, and therefore we do earnestly wish we might be so happy as to find a remedy before it be too late for us to contribute to our own deliverance; but although these be our wishes yet we will by no means put your Highness into any expectations which may misguide your own counsels in this matter, so that the best advice we can give is to inform your Highness truly both of the state of things here at this time and of the difficulties which appear to us. As to the first, the people are so generally dissatisfied with the present conduct of the Government in relation to their religion, liberties, and properties (all which have been greatly invaded), and they are in such expectation of their prospects being daily worse that your Highness may be assured there are nineteen parts of twenty of the people throughout the Kingdom who are desirous of a change.' Signed 25 24 27 29 31 35 33.

William of Orange had previously been given the codes and knew who had written to him: the Earl of Shrewsbury code 25, the Earl of Devon code 24, the Earl of Danby code 27, Viscount Lumley code 29, Edward Compton, the Bishop of London code 31, Edward Russell code 35 and Henry Sidney code 33. Knowing that the chance of his and his wife Mary's succession to the throne was lost with the birth of a son to James II, William now agreed to help and put together his massive invading army and navy all paid for out of William's own purse, but with huge support from the people of the Netherlands. He would come to England with those words on the Brixham statue on his lips:

'The Liberties of England and the Protestant Religion, I will maintain.'

CHAPTER 3

SOME RESEARCH SOURCES

We know much about William of Orange's preparations and voyage from the Netherlands to Brixham and about his march to London because there were many individuals that travelled with him who wrote accounts that thankfully, still exist. Examples of research sources are:

Rev John Whittle

William had several chaplains who accompanied him and his army. One, the Rev John Whittle kept a diary carefully detailing the Prince's journey from his Palace in The Hague to his landing at Brixham and the march to London. Its full title is:

'An exact diary of the late expedition of his Illustrious Highness the Prince of Orange (now the King of Great Britain) from his palace at The Hague to his landing in Torbay. And from thence to his arrival at Whitehall, giving a particular account of all that happened and every day's march.'

At the beginning of his diary which was published in 1689 there is an interesting Devon connection. John Whittle dedicated his diary to four prominent men including Sir John Maynard (1604-1690). He was a Devonian and had been an MP for Totnes, Plymouth, Exeter and Bere Alston from 1640 to 1690, Recorder at both Plymouth and Totnes and had held senior positions in Parliament. He was a member of the committee that designed the Declaration of Rights in 1689. Its outcome was clear guidelines to regulate relations between Parliament and the Crown that had been sorely lacking up to that point in time.

William Bentinck

William Bentinck, who became the 1st Earl of Portland, was the mastermind behind the invasion and William's chief advisor. His documents were given to the University of Nottingham by one of his descendants and some are available online at the University of Nottingham Manuscripts and Special Collections learning resource 'Conflict'. For example, one document is the 'Order of March' and it helpfully maps out the route that William of Orange and his troops took from Brixham to London.

Dr Gilbert Burnet

William's personal chaplain was Dr Gilbert Burnet (1643-1715). He wrote 'History of His Own Time' which was published in 1724. It covers the period of English history from 1660 to 1715. This book and an anonymous letter attributed to Dr Burnet have much about William's expedition. Being William of Orange's personal chaplain and therefore closer to him than John Whittle, Dr Burnet includes some details about the decisions made about where to land and those made en route. Dr Burnet had been apprehensive when James II came to the throne and he fled to France and then settled in the Netherlands. William of Orange invited him to The Hague and appointed him as his chaplain for the expedition to England. He was rewarded by being made Bishop of Salisbury in 1689.

Celia Fiennes

Another late 17th-century writer was Celia Fiennes (1662-1741). She was born in Newton Toney near Salisbury, the daughter of a colonel in Cromwell's army. She grew up to be a staunch Non-Conformist and was a supporter of William of Orange. Between 1685 and 1712 she travelled up and down the length and breadth of England. In 1698, she passed through Devon on her way to Cornwall. She encountered the same travelling difficulties as William and his marching army. Her diaries provide interesting insights into the Devonshire countryside, the hustle and bustle of Exeter, and her opinions of Honiton and Axminster.

Constantijn Huygens

Constantijn Huygens was the personal secretary of William of Orange and like Dr Burnet was close to him. Like John Whittle his diary also includes fascinating snippets about what took place in the Netherlands, the voyage to Brixham and at every town and city in the march through Devon.

Oral Histories

There are also the oral histories handed down over the generations to family and friends that add a local flavour to his journey. Many of these were mentioned in lectures presented to the Devonshire Association in the latter part of the 19th century.

CHAPTER 4

THE PREPARATIONS FOR THE JOURNEY FROM THE NETHERLANDS

That question: Why did William of Orange choose to land at Brixham? The simple answer is that he didn't. At least, not to start with because he had no fixed or preconceived idea about where to land other than it would be on the east coast of England or its south coast. So, prior to sailing, William of Orange instructed William Bentinck to survey both the south coast and east coast of England.

The survey was very detailed and listed the ports and possible landing places, the distance between the various locations and the number of rivers that would have to be crossed, plus comments about their suitability. For example, Lyme Regis where the Duke of Monmouth landed with his three ships and 86 men on his failed bid for the throne in 1685 was deemed a difficult place to land for 500 ships and 15,000 soldiers.

Torbay was certainly not the first choice, and it was noted that Torbay: 'can only be defended with difficulty'. It also points out that the distance between Exmouth and Torbay is 15 miles and after a landing at Torbay the march to Exeter would involve crossing two rivers, the Exe and the Teign. Dartmouth however, was thought to be better place to land as: 'a landing is possible on both banks' of the River Dart.

Figure 4 – the mouth of the River Dart (image Rowena Coote)

A march from Kingswear on the east bank from the River Dart would be as straightforward as one from Brixham, whereas a march from the west bank of the River Dart at Dartmouth would be (as it is today) a slow journey to Totnes and then on to Newton Abbot. William Bentinck's original survey is one of the documents held at the 'University of Nottingham Manuscripts and Special Collections': reference number Pw A 2188/8.

Henry Sidney, the author and signatory of the invitation to William, travelled to The Hague to discuss the planned invasion. His advice was a) to come with a large fleet, but a small army because a large army would suggest a conquest, b) to land in the North of England which had horses and good roads and c) not to land in the West of England where memories of the failure of the Monmouth Rebellion and the punishment of those involved at the Bloody Assizes might discourage support for his cause. Furthermore, others proposed that the prince should divide his force, land himself with a greater part in the North, and send a detachment under Marshall Schoenberg in the West.

William could not agree to Sidney's advice and proposals. He would bring a large army, sufficient horses and one month's food because he had to be prepared for the worst scenario, not knowing if the army of James II would defect to him. He did not want to make the same mistakes as his cousin, the Duke of Monmouth, who in June 1685 made his own unsuccessful and disastrous claim on the throne. He also sailed from the Netherlands but with just three ships and 86 men, landed at Lyme Regis and was dependent right from the start on support of the local population, the landed gentry and noblemen.

Furthermore, Admiral Herbert, the commander-in-chief of William's fleet, was against landing in the north because of its dangerous coastline at that time of the year and believed that the English Channel was a safer alternative. This then was the plan: to sail down the English Channel and land somewhere on the south coast of England.

After choosing the regiments and the soldiers that he would take to England, William ordered that the men-of-war (the warships) should 'at all speed be made ready to sail to England'. Ships from Rotterdam, Dort, Delph, Leyden, Harlem and other cities took up the challenge and the fleet assembled off the city of Brill. Merchant ships and other boats were hired to carry soldiers, horses, ammunition and provisions. John Whittle estimated that there were just over 400 ships including 50 men-of-war and over 300 transport ships. These were needed to carry the one month's supply of food and fodder. Later in his diary, Whittle suggests that the number of ships could be nearer to 500. By early October William's invasion plan was taking shape.

William Bentinck's 'Plan of the fleet' is also held by the University of Nottingham (Reference Pw A 2197/2). It gives a feel for the brilliant organisation that went into the invasion, names some of those who were sailing in each of the ships and who was in command of each squadron of between 24 and 30 ships. There were for example, English Lords, Scottish Lords, English Gentleman and English soldiers sailing with William of Orange who had fled England the year before being in fear of their lives from the death threats of James II. They would have known who the Protestants and Roman Catholics were right across the country including those in Devon and therefore those who William of Orange could trust. There were also 20 English pilots ensuring a landing could be made almost anywhere along the English coast.

But during his preparation stage things did not go all William of Orange's way. When the ships were off Brill, the wind turned to a northerly and a huge storm battered the ships for days. William ordered that the small ships should shelter in the harbour whilst the larger ships sailed to Zeeland, the westernmost province of the Netherlands hoping that it would be a safer place to ride out the storm. Whilst most of the larger ships weathered the storm, some were damaged and limped into Goeree south of Hellevoetsluis for repairs. Meanwhile the troops were now ordered to get to the fleet and be prepared to board ship. But the storm continued for many days and John Whittle writes:

'One night the Winds were so very high, and the Air so tempestuous and stormy, shaking the very Houses and People in their Beds, insomuch that many judged it to be a Earthquake; the whole Fleet was in great peril... Every morning the very first question was asked... Sir, I pray how is the Wind today? Are we likely to get an Easterly Wind ere long? Pray God send it, and such like.'

The mood was at times gloomy. There was concern that the weather might continue to turn against them again with the consequence of not being able to sail until after the winter.

Meanwhile, back in England, James II was praying that the northerly and westerly winds would continue until Christmas and hence delaying the departure of William's fleet until the better weather of the spring of the following year.

CHAPTER 5

THE VOYAGE FROM THE NETHERLANDS TO ENGLAND

19 OCTOBER 1688 - THE FLEET DEPARTS FROM THE NETHERLANDS

By 14 October the weather was improving and the wind, says Constantijn Huygens, had turned to a south-easterly and the fleet was expecting to sail. He arrived at Hellevoetsluis on 17 October where he saw the fleet being repaired and prepared for the voyage. John Whittle writes again about the weather and the preparations:

'After some time that the Weather had been so tempestuous, it began for to settle, and God sent us an East Wind, to the exceeding great joy of all our hearts in Holland. Everything was sent to the Fleet, as Provision for one month, the Artillery, Magazine, Powder, Ball, Match, Tents, Tent-poles, Stocking-axes, Spades, and all sorts of Utensils convenient in War; and then Hay and Pro vender for the Horses, Fresh Water, and a hundred things more, which do not now occur to my memory. The Wind continuing East. The Horses began to be shipp'd at Rotterdam.'

The ships were then loaded with the horses and one month's provision. Lord Mordaunt, the man who would have a key role in paving the way for William of Orange to enter Exeter came aboard ship and William Bentinck read letters from England explaining of the great reluctance amongst the English Navy to attack. This was good news and at last the fleet felt confident enough to set sail. The letter was probably one of many sent from England to William of Orange in code or in invisible ink to maintain the secrecy of the intelligence it contained.

The fleet finally left the Netherlands on 19 October 1688, but on the second day of their voyage, the wind turned to a westerly and another storm developed with very high seas and lightning. The ships were driven in all directions: some towards the coast of England, others in a northerly direction and some ships rode out the storm at anchor.

The fleet, one-by-one trickled back into the harbours for safety and repairs. 1,300 horses had been lost: many had died on board ship, whilst others had been thrown overboard. William ordered Admiral Herbert to assess the status of the fleet and ordered him to keep the ships with horses at Hellevoetsluis, but those with the infantry to be kept close to his own ship. He was keen to set sail with the protection of his army as soon as the wind permitted it.

In fact, William, says John Whittle was not in the least dismayed. Despite the weather, despite the time of year and the setbacks and delays, he was undaunted in his task ahead. But says Huygens, the wind was now 'a nasty northwest' and many thought the expedition would have to wait until the spring of the following year.

A few days later an English ship arrived and informed Dr Burnet that the English fleet would never fight the Dutch fleet and had drunk to the Prince of Orange's health. Was this message genuine or was it propaganda sent by James II to trick William into bringing a smaller army and a smaller fleet? William would not of course change his plans because the army of James II was, according to Dr Burnet: 'when all together was reckoned about 30,000 strong'. William of Orange would soon find out the scale of the opposition to him!

1 NOVEMBER 1688 – THE FLEET DEPARTS A SECOND TIME

Eleven days later, the storm had abated, the repairs to the ships had been finished and fresh horses were on board and, says John Whittle, 'the Protestant wind blew'. In other words the wind had turned to a fresh and brisk easterly. He continues:

'The Prince of Orange hearing thereof, and seeing the Wind blow so fresh, was fully resolv'd (by the blessing of God) to set to sea on the morrow.'

William ordered that the fleet should set sail on the evening tide of 1 November 1688 and it headed for the south coast of England. Warships sailed at the head of the fleet to protect not only William but also the transport ships from any attacks from the English fleet. Despite sailing day and night, progress was deliberately slow in order to allow the huge fleet to catch up. John Whittle explains how the layout of the fleet demonstrated more of the extraordinary organisation and planning that went into the voyage:

'The whole Fleet was divided into three Squadrons; the Red Flag was for the English and Scotch, commanded by Major-General Mackay; the White Flag was for the Prince's Guards, and the Brandenburghers, commanded by Count Solms; the Blue Flag was for the Dutch and French, commanded by Count Nassau. Now every Ship had a certain Mark or Token, that it might be known unto what Squadron she belong'd.'

Admiral Herbert, the commander-in-chief of William's fleet, was in the centre of the huge flotilla with his own standard or distinguishing flag. It had taken until daybreak of 2 November for all the ships to set sail. During this time William himself was some 15 or so miles out to sea on board the ship 'The Brill' flying a flag in the English colours on which his motto was clearly written: 'The Protestant Religion and Liberties of England. And I will Maintain it.'

3 NOVEMBER 1688 – THE STRAIT OF DOVER

On 3 November it was realised that some ships were lost from the fleet and they were in the cannon sights of the English ships which lay at anchor off modern-day Southend-on-Sea at Gunfleet. They turned back in a hurry as the English fired cannon shots and damaged one ship which was captured. The others sailed on with William of Orange.

He held a Council of War with his Admirals and ordered that three frigates should sail to the mouth of the River Thames to assess the strength and position of the English Navy. They reported that 34 ships lay in that area. Learning this concerning news, William instigated a plan to protect his fleet. He ordered that it stretched in a line to within three miles of the coasts of Dover and Calais, be 25 deep and the rear and flanks be guarded by the men-of-war.

On Saturday 3 November, the ships passed through the Strait of Dover discovering, says Constantijn Huygens: 'the high white mountains of England' and in the evening the crews could see the huge crowds lining the Kent cliffs. The sights that day were spectacular for both the spectators on the shore and the crews on the ships. John Whittle writes:

'The People both at Dover and Calais having discover'd the Fleet, were amaz'd at such a glorious Sight, yet formidable Navie, insomuch that all the convenient places for beholding us, were much throng'd, especially in and about Dover.'

The crews also noticed that the fire beacons had been lit to warn those living on the coast of the approach of an enemy. The beacons stretched inland too and would have informed James II of the arrival of William of Orange in English waters.

4 NOVEMBER 1688 – THE BIRTHDAY OF WILLIAM OF ORANGE

The next day being Sunday 4 November was both William's birthday and his wedding anniversary which he celebrated off the Isle of Wight which they had reached by 9 am. It was also an opportunity for any straggling ships to catch up with the fleet and most on board assumed that they would land that day on the Isle of Wight or at nearby Portsmouth, but they were mistaken. Others, says Dr Burnet: 'thought that the following day being 'gunpowder treason day' would most sensibly affect the English'.

William thinking that Portsmouth was heavily defended ordered the fleet to set sail at 4 pm and it made good progress sailing farther down the English Channel. Whittle describes the amazing sight of 500 ships lit up at night and the favourable weather as they sailed west:

'It was no ordinary sight, for to behold the Seas all cover'd with Lights, the Lanthorns appearing at a distance like unto so many Stars in the Water, dancing to and fro, here and there, according to the motion of the Ship; but above all, the Cabin of that Vessel wherein the Prince was, having so many Wax Lights burning within it, glittered most gloriously, it seem'd a Paradise for pleasure and delight.

The Wind was very favourable, and blowed very fresh, which caused our whole Fleet to plow the curling Waves, and cross the appeased Seas, with very good speed and pleasure.'

By the evening the fleet had rounded Portland Bill and William ordered that two frigates and three of the ships carrying infantry must proceed towards Dartmouth to seize the two castles which defended the port in order to ensure his safe entry. These were Dartmouth Castle on the west bank of the mouth of the River Dart and Kingswear Castle on its east bank and both were formidable defences.

Perhaps William really was intending to land at Dartmouth and Kingswear and not at Brixham. He and his advisors had remembered the notes in William Bentinck's survey of the coastline: 'Torbay can only be defended with difficulty and at Dartmouth a landing is possible on both banks of the River Dart.' On the other hand, Torbay was thought the safer anchorage for such a huge fleet.

CHAPTER 6

THE LANDING AT BRIXHAM

5 NOVEMBER 1688 - WILLIAM OF ORANGE ARRIVES AT BRIXHAM

During the night of 4 November and the early morning of 5 November, the fleet had sailed past Exmouth, it had sailed past Teignmouth and all or some of the fleet had sailed past Torbay on the easterly wind. It was a foggy and misty morning and the fleet found themselves close to a rocky shoreline that was a 'stone's throw away'. Not only were they unsure where they were, they could not find a place to land.

The fleet had sailed close to Berry Head, the southern tip of Torbay and continued in a south-westerly direction towards the mouth of the River Dart. That six-mile stretch of coastline from Berry Head at Brixham to the mouth of the River Dart has changed little over the centuries. Other than a few coves, behind which are fields, it is a continuous stretch of high cliffs that are totally unsuitable for the landing of a huge army, its horses and its supplies.

Figure 5 – the high cliffs between Torbay and the mouth of the River Dart

This is how John Whittle describes the morning:

'So when the day began to dawn, we found that we were very near the English Shore, but whereabout we could not yet tell. The Ship in which the Prince of

Orange was, sailed so near the Shore, that with much facility a man might cast a Stone on the Land; we were driven very slowly, all our Sails being struck. The Morning was very obscure with the Fog and Mist, and withal it was so calm, that the Vessels now as 'twere touch'd each other; every Ship coming as near unto the Ship wherein the Prince of Orange was, as the Skipper thereof would permit them. Here we were moving for a while very slowly by the Shore, and could see all the Rocks thereabouts very plain. We perceived that we should land thereabout, but no place near was commodious for either Men or Horses, it being a steep Rock to march up.'

Dr Burnet also gives an interesting insight to the day. He says that at noon on 4 November, the best of all the English pilots came aboard his ship and was given orders to sail so that next morning the fleet should be short of Dartmouth. The intention was for some of the ships to land there because news arrived that the English Fleet was not stationed there and that the rest should sail into Torbay. The pilot made one or more navigation errors and says Burnet: 'we were passed Torbay and Dartmouth'. There was a real fear that the fleet would have to sail on to Plymouth for a frosty reception and a long and tedious campaign in winter.

However, the easterly wind suddenly changed direction. John Whittle continues: 'It pleased God of heaven' to give a westerly wind and the fleet was blown into Torbay. The 'Protestant' east wind had brought the fleet from the Netherlands and the west wind allowed the ships to turn around at some point southwest of Torbay and enter its waters. The entire fleet was in Torbay by 3 pm of the afternoon of 5 November 1688.

The plan to march quickly from Torbay to Exeter and make it their headquarters was back on track.

William then ordered the whole fleet into the same format as at Dover and Calais, whilst the smaller men-of-war were to guard the landing and the Admirals should stand out at sea with six men-of-war to guard Torbay.

The sun then rose over the calm sea and the mist evaporated to give a fine day. The bells of St Mary's Church in Brixham were ringing and William thought the bells were welcoming him, but of course this was not the case. Being 5 November they were being rung to celebrate the anniversary of the overthrow of the Gunpowder Plot of 1605.

Nearing Brixham, William ordered that the fleet flew a white flag uppermost to signify peace, but a red flag below to signify war to those who opposed him. And as his ships sailed close to the cliffs at Brixham, the locals came out in droves to the sides and brows of its hills to watch the spectacle of nearly 500 ships entering the bay. Another of William's ministers shouted from the highest cabin of the ship the 'Golden Sun': 'It is the Prince of Orange that comes for the Protestant Religion'. As he shouted he pulled a bible out of his pocket, he opened it and holding it in his right hand, made many flourishes with it towards the crowds.

William ordered that the fleet should come to anchor and his army should land immediately. His ship was in the middle of the bay. He was protected by two men-of-war sailing in front of his vessel, and one on each side. General Mackay with his six Regiments of English and Scots soldiers landed first to assess the strength of any opposition, protected by a ship with eighteen guns. But there was no opposition, in fact it was quite the opposite, for, says Dr Burnet:

'the people bid us heartily welcome to England; and gave us all manner of provisions for our refreshment... for both for man and horse and were paid their price honestly for it.'

Then, Count Solms and the ten or twelve grenadiers who were William's personal bodyguard stepped safely ashore. Knowing that there was definitely no opposition, William transferred from his flagship the Harleian Miscellany to the smaller Princess Mary, named after his wife and sailed towards Brixham's harbour inlet. He then climbed into a barge that would take him towards the harbour's old stone pier.

His arrival on English soil would, he thought, be a triumph. Since leaving the Netherlands on 1 November all had gone to plan. But at Brixham that afternoon, it was low tide and his barge became stuck in the mud of Brixham Harbour. This inauspicious start to the invasion was though, an opportunity for a Brixham man to make a name for himself. It was the fisherman Peter Varwell who dashed down the steps of the old stone pier, waded through the sticky harbour mud and its murky harbour water to the barge and carried the Prince safely to shore. It's quite amazing that a humble Brixham fisherman, a Devonian, carried a future monarch on to English soil. An alternative version of this story is that when becoming stuck in the Brixham mud, another Brixham man by the name of Youldon called out to William: 'You'm welcome', to which William of Orange replied that if he was welcome, could someone carry him to shore.

As late as the 1930s a Brixham school teacher Miss Varwell, a descendant of Peter Varwell told her pupils of her ancestor's brave act.

The Varwell family tradition is that Peter Varwell rode his pony in front of the Prince all the way to London where he was rewarded with £100 and used the money to build a new home. This story also has another version which suggests that Peter Varwell rode only as far as Exeter and was given a letter of authority to claim the £100 pounds reward if he was ever in London. Sometime later he did travel to the capital. Stopping at an inn, he had too much to drink, bragged about his letter which was then stolen and the thief claimed the £100. Peter Varwell went to the Palace himself to claim the reward but was sent packing.

Figure 6 – Brixham Harbour at low tide

The Brixham Heritage Museum archive throws more light about who carried William of Orange ashore at Brixham and contains three other accounts. It mentions a letter dated 13 February 1693 by Thomas Dobbins, captain and previously a gunner on HMS Nonsuch, that states: 'I am the person who carried the king from his barge at Torbay', whilst Sir William Phips, Governor of Massachusetts, in a letter to Lord Nottingham on 15 February 1693 notifying Thomas Dobbin's appointment as captain on the Nonsuch writes: 'he is the same person that carried the king at Torbay'. The Brixham Heritage Museum archive also quotes from the book 'Tours in the West through Devon and Cornwall', published in 1800, in which the author, M Hansford, explains that whilst he was in Brixham, a well-dressed and elderly man took him to the harbour steps where William of Orange landed. The man said this to M Hansford:

'I am 70 years old, and the tradition from my grandmother who died many years since at a great age was about 18 years old when the Prince of Orange and his fleet came into Torbay... She stood at this place and saw three men take the prince out of the boat, the tide being out, and carry him over the mud to these landing steps. He put his foot on that blue stone with the white vein. The Prince gave nothing to the men until he was crowned king, when he sent for the person at whose house he lodged in Brixham and bountifully rewarded him.'

This oral history story is another confirmation that the future monarch was indeed carried ashore by one or more persons and takes nothing away from the Brixham tradition about Peter Varwell. It makes complete sense that more than one person carried William of Orange through the thick, slippery and deep mud of the harbour because to do this singlehandedly would have been hazardous and put William's life in danger. It is also confirmation that William rewarded Peter Varwell, in whose house he slept in on his first night in England.

After stepping ashore, William, with several Lords and Gentlemen marched up 'the hill' says John Whittle from where they could see the fleet approaching the harbour and the men-of-war sailing up and down the length of the bay providing protection. Constantijn Huygens describes this hill as: 'as a mountain with short rows of houses dotted here and there'. Both he and Whittle were referring to the steep hill now named Overgang that is behind the current Brixham fish market. The word 'gang' means passageway in Dutch and the hill may well have been named after the arrival of William of Orange. In 1688 however, there was no road up that hill - just a muddy track of red Devon soil.

John Whittle describes the view from the top of Overgang and the hive of activity on the quayside to bring the men, horses and supplies ashore:

'The Navy was like a little City, the Masts appearing like so many Spires and the People were like Bees swarming all over the Bay. Extraordinary pains was now taken, by all sorts of Men, to get their necessary things to Shore.'

The soldiers were so eager to come ashore, some having been on board for well over two weeks and had endured the storms off the coast of the Netherlands. They crowded onto the barges from where some jumped overboard and found themselves in water that was anything from up to their knees to up to their ears. However, bearing in mind that the fleet arrived in the afternoon, the unloading continued during the evening and night. The officers and soldiers were constantly marching up Overgang with drums beating and colours flying and the army camped in the fields in the area of Brixham now known as Furzeham. Dr Burnet estimated that by the end of the day 2,000 soldiers had landed and the disembarkation continued on 6 and 7 November. To maintain order, each regiment camped in a different field surrounded by a high Devon hedge or stone wall. John Whittle describes the November weather:

'It was a cold frosty Night, and the Stars twinkl'd exceedingly; besides, the Ground was very wet after so much Rain and ill Weather; the Souldiers were to stand to their Arms the whole Night, at least to be all in a readiness if anything should happen, or the Enemy make an Assault.'

The soldiers collected firewood from the hedgerows and no doubt from the nearby ancient Grove Wood that still exists on the outskirts of that side of Brixham.

After inspecting his army and fleet, William of Orange returned from Furzeham to the harbour area and spent the evening and night in Peter Varwell's fisherman's cottage in Middle Street with a strong guard surrounding it. During the evening he would, no doubt have held a strategy meeting with his generals to plan the march from Brixham to Exeter where he intended to make his temporary headquarters.

Peter Varwell's cottage was ideally situated being very near to the harbour and his fleet, and near to his army camping high up at Furzeham. Unfortunately though, Peter Varwell's house was bombed and destroyed during World War II. All the Lords, says John Whittle, were quartered in fishermen's cottages.

The nearby alehouse was understandably very busy and crowded that evening, and the landlord, whilst it seems he ran out of ale and bread, 'strutted about as if indeed he had been a Lord himself, because he was honoured with Lords Company'. Huygens mentions the Crowned Rose Tavern, full of soldiers drinking, and was where he had a mattress in an upstairs room to sleep on after a meal of mutton stew.

There was concern about how to land the horses quickly and effectively so William asked the fishermen to direct his men to the most convenient place for landing the horses. The following morning they were taken to a cove that was a quarter-of-a-mile from the town. This was probably Fishcombe Cove which is a short distance along the coastline from the harbour. Here the ships could be brought very near to land where the horses would not need to swim more than 20 yards. The sea was dead calm that morning and the horses were quickly landed but, like the soldiers, were not able to 'find their legs' for some days.

One oral history passed down the generations was to Edward Windeatt, the Town Clerk of Totnes, in 1880. An 80-year-old Brixham man, had recalled to him the stories handed down over three or four generations. A Captain Clements had told this Brixham man that he had heard seven or eight old men explain to him that whilst a few horses came ashore at the quayside, the majority were thrown overboard and guided by a single rope tied to the ships and to the shore.

The artillery, magazine, and heavy baggage were left on board ship and taken to Topsham on the River Exe where it would meet up with the army at Exeter.

The disembarkation of soldiers, horses and the one month's supply of food for both men and horses took two days. Lighter equipment was unloaded in Brixham's inlet at high tide and ships and barges formed a bridge to speed up the unloading, whilst some troops disembarked at Paignton. What a hive of activity and what a scene it must have been. It was a masterpiece in logistics and must have been an extraordinary sight on this most extraordinary of days in Brixham.

The Torquay Directory newspaper of 19 July 1899 printed the contents of a letter, dated 6 November 1688, from William of Orange to Admiral Herbert who was overseeing the fleet and coordinating the movements of the men-of-war. William writes that he has no news about the whereabouts of the English Fleet and asks Admiral Herbert to continue the protection of the fleet in Torbay. He also asks for his advice as to: 'the best means of sending back to Holland all the transport ships as soon as they have been unloaded and what is to be done with the fleet'. He then instructs Herbert to arrange for two regiments to be taken to Topsham so that they can march to Exeter and rendezvous with Lord Mordaunt and Dr Burnet who also went ahead of William to Exeter from Newton Abbot.

According to Dr Burnet the fleet of James II had been in pursuit when, off the Isle of Wight, the wind turned and developed into a storm. His ships limped into Portsmouth which says Dr Burnet: 'will not be fit for service that year'. Dr Burnet, a chaplain, interpreted the changes in the wind for the voyage: the east wind that brought the fleet from the Netherlands, the west wind off the mouth of the River Dart which allowed the fleet to turn around and enter Torbay and the storm encountered by James II's fleet, as the hand and protection of God. The series of circumstances were certainly remarkable.

So where exactly did the Prince of Orange step onto English soil in Brixham Harbour? The harbour at Brixham was different in the 17th century from what it is in the early 21st century. Brixham had an inlet, which is now reclaimed land that extended at least a quarter of a mile up the valley alongside Fore Street. The inlet was therefore, large and substantial enough to form a useful shelter for the small fishing fleet with the water being eight feet deep at high tide. An old stone pier was located where the inlet joined the harbour at the spot where the old fish market stands, and hence very near to both the location of the statue of William Orange and where the replica of the Golden Hind is moored. It is on the steps of this old stone pier with its 'blue stone with the white vein' that William most likely first set foot in England.

There is another monument in Brixham erected in 1830 to commemorate the arrival of William of Orange. Its current location – having been moved at least twice – is alongside the old fish market. It has an inscription on it that reads: 'On this spot and near this place William Prince of Orange first set foot on his landing in England fifth November 1688'. It's a conundrum.

Figure 7 – the first Brixham monument to William of Orange erected in 1830

How could William of Orange set foot both on the spot where the monument is and also near to it? The monument is some way from the old stone pier. The answer is simple. In or around 1830, the old stone pier, the place of William's landing, was dismantled probably when the inlet was being reclaimed and the granite steps of that pier – those very steps on which William stood on his arrival - were used to make the base of this monument.

Word of the arrival of William of Orange travelled fast and John Whittle wrote: 'many people from all the adjacent places came flocking to see the Prince of Orange'. Who were these people?

Nicholas Roope was a member of the rich and influential Roope family in Dartmouth and is believed to be one who welcomed the Prince at Brixham. Four years later in 1692, Roope wrote to the Earl of Nottingham about an incident at Dartmouth and informs him that: 'I was the first gentleman who went into the king and I have served him faithfully since, and shall do ...' He was the first to pledge allegiance to William which, bearing in mind the terrible fate of those loyal to the Duke of Monmouth at Exeter in 1685 at the Bloody Assizes, was an extremely brave act in the early days of William's invasion.

Another who greeted William was Sir Edward Seymour of Berry Pomeroy Castle who afterwards invited him to a property on his estate. Rawlyn Mallock, the squire of nearby Cockington Court near Torquay who was a staunch Protestant was also at Brixham, as was the son of Sir William Courtenay of Forde House in Newton Abbot who invited William to lodge at his home on his way to Exeter.

Other well-wishers included Samuel Windeatt, a strict nonconformist and his eight-year-old son Thomas who rode from Totnes to Brixham. On their return they told stories about the country folk bringing apples for the soldiers. For example, an oral history in the family of T W Windeatt, who presented a Devonshire Association lecture in 1880 about William of Orange, is about Will Webber of Staverton who, as a boy, went with his father with a cart load of apples to the high road between Brixham and Exeter where the soldiers could help themselves. This was another brave act in those fearful times. T W Windeatt also mentions that twelve-year-old Juliana Babbage of Totnes in the company of an old lady walked to Brixham, where William shook hands with them and gave them some of his proclamations to distribute.

CHAPTER 7

THE MARCH FROM BRIXHAM TO EXETER

6 NOVEMBER 1688 - BRIXHAM TO PAIGNTON

When William of Orange woke up on 6 November 1688, he must have been extremely pleased with his progress thus far.

The voyage had been incident free and the landing at Brixham was, despite the harbour mud, a triumph. There had been no opposition whatsoever and he was welcomed by the people of Brixham and those from further afield. The logistics of unloading of men, horses and supplies was a success too. John Whittle confirms the size of the army:

'The Number of his Highness's Regiments landed here at this Bay, was about six and twenty, the number of Officers about one thousand, the number of Field - Officers about seventy eight: The number of all his Forces and Soldiers about fifteen thousand four hundred and odd Men.'

However, a new day meant new challenges and William was more than keen to commence the march from Brixham to Paignton and then on to Newton Abbot using the routes discussed with his advisors the previous evening in the home of Peter Varwell.

The night had been cold and frosty and it is said that on waking up in the morning, the soldiers found themselves covered in red Devon mud. Walking up steep, muddy Overgang the day before must have been a shock to those used to the flat Dutch countryside and there were more surprises to come as the soldiers and horses commenced their march.

The Rev Whittle mentions in his diary that the army marched on 6 November to Paignton in the dark and must therefore have departed from Brixham late afternoon when the winter daylight was fading fast. John Whittle's description of the march is enlightening:

'This first day we marched some hours after Night in the Dark and Rain; the Lanes hereabout were very narrow, and not used to Wagons, Carts or Coaches, and therefore extremely rough and stony, which hindered us very much from making any speed... As we marched here upon good Ground, the Soldiers would stumble and sometimes fall, because of a dizziness in their Heads after they had been so long toss'd at Sea, the very Ground seem'd to roll up and down for some days, according to the manner of the Waves.'

South Devon soil is predominately red clay soil and after rain, the unmetalled lanes even today become very soft, muddy and slippery. Pot holes and dips in the lanes and paths still fill up with rainwater producing muddy puddles and walking through them on foot can result in wet feet.

Many lanes of Devon in the late 17th century were particularly muddy and narrow because Devon farmers used pack horses rather than horse and cart, so there was little need for the lanes to be faced with stone or chippings. In fact, wheels were not in use on Devon farms until 1770. In addition, some lanes were and still are steep and full of sharp, irregular shaped stones of up to six inches in diameter which are particularly hard going on foot. In 1698, Celia Fiennes described a Devon lane as: 'full of stones and dirt for the most part and because they are so close, the sun and wind cannot come to them.' A good example is Fleet Mill Lane that connects the hamlet of Aish and the outskirts of Totnes which continues to be a lane as described by John Whittle and Celia Fiennes. These then, were the conditions of the roads that William and his army experienced on their march to Paignton and beyond.

Figure 8 – the muddy and stony Fleet Mill Lane in South Devon

Their route to Paignton was through Churston and Goodrington and their horses, pulling carts of fodder and supplies soon became stuck in the mud and ruts of Devon's lanes. Progress was extremely hard and slow. So why had no one warned them about the awful condition of Devon's roads? Then, reaching Paignton the army met up with those who had disembarked there the day before.

Their second night at or in the vicinity of Paignton was no better than the first night. Despite it being very stormy and raining hard many of the soldiers slept in the open air, sinking into the soft, wet clay soil with fires lit using wood from hedges and gates to provide some warmth. The morning brought a little respite when a field of turnips was discovered which were eaten raw or roasted over the fires to provide some sustenance before the next day's march. However, William of Orange had not accompanied the army on their march to Paignton. He had other business to attend to.

During the morning of 6 November, whilst the army was preparing to march away from Brixham, William's secretary Constantijn Huygens was busy writing letters. Then at midday, William ordered Huygens to follow him and his infantry on horseback to a secret location, but because his horse was still on board ship, he was unable to do so. He was delayed until half-past-three by which time, he and those still in Brixham, had no idea as to where William had ridden to. William's cousin, Major-General William Frederick Zuylestein, sent Huygens to 'King's-Castel', thinking that William might be there. This was in all probability Kingswear Castle situated at the mouth of the River Dart and the most secure building in the locality. However, it was a fool's errand because, later on, Huygens heard that William was at Paignton. So to where did William of Orange ride on the afternoon of 6 November 1688?

Whilst the army were marching to Paignton, William took the opportunity to meet other influential Protestants. Brixham tradition is that Peter Varwell took him via Churston to a thatched cottage now called King William Cottage that is situated very near to the Paignton recycling centre at Yalberton. From there he was guided to Aish (a hamlet near the village of Stoke Gabriel) and then on to a house in a secluded valley in the hamlet of Longcombe that is midway between Paignton and Totnes. Celia Fiennes's 1698 description of the isolated properties in rural Devon explain why William of Orange needed the services of a guide:

'On these hills one can discern little besides enclosures, hedge and trees, rarely can one see houses unless you are just descending to them, they always are placed in holes as it were and you have a precipice to go down to come at them.'

Being midway between Totnes and Paignton, Longcombe was a great location for William to meet dignitaries and others who had heard the reports of his arrival. And being tucked in the bottom of a valley it could be easily defended. Longcombe was also part of Sir Edward Seymour's Berry Pomeroy estate and this visit was to a thatched house that still exists and is now called 'Parliament House'.

Figure 9 – Parliament House, Longcombe

But why did Sir Edward Seymour not invite William to nearby Berry Pomeroy Castle? The explanation is this. Edward Seymour was part way through an ambitious building programme at the castle that had commenced in 1600 by his forebears, but had stalled and was not finished. So it would have been too embarrassing to invite a future monarch with the builders there. In fact, Berry Pomeroy Castle was abandoned sometime between 1688 and 1701 and become the picturesque ruin it is today.

The Ordnance Survey map for the area has at the location of Parliament House the word 'Parliament'. William of Orange held his first Parliament on English soil in South Devon at Longcombe. Those attending this 'Parliament' would have included influential South Devon Protestants who had encouraged him to come to England, and no doubt some ex-members of the Town Council in Totnes who had fallen out of favour with James II. To commemorate this occasion there is a memorial stone in the front garden of Parliament House which reads: 'William of Orange is said to have held his first parliament here in November 1688'. It was erected in the 19th-century by the Seymour Estate.

Did William sleep at Parliament House on the night of 6 November? The Rev Whittle writes in his diary that William: 'went unto a certain Gentleman's House and lodged there, his own guards being with him', and this could indeed be Parliament House. Constantijn Huygens writes that it rained hard that night and he slept in the vicinity of Paignton (perhaps at Longcombe) in a tent whilst others including William Bentinck had the misery of camping in the open.

Some Paignton historians support the theory that William slept in Paignton itself. The logic is that William would want to reunite with both his army and his secretary who had marched from Brixham to Paignton and had joined forces with those who had landed at Paignton. The whole invasion force would then be ready for the march to Newton Abbot the following day on 7 November.

If the Paignton historians are correct, then William would most likely have stayed overnight in Church Street at the Old Posting House, later renamed the Crown and Sceptre, then the Crown and Anchor. T W Windeatt refers to the Prince sleeping in the Crown and Anchor Inn in which a bedroom was named later the 'Prince's Room'. The inn was known in an 1825 sketch as the 'King's Castle' but was this a name taken from Constantijn Huygens's diary to help create a Paignton legend that William of Orange slept in Paignton? The building, albeit rebuilt since those times, still exists and has an archway that led to the stables at the rear and is now a short cut for pedestrians and light traffic from Church Street to Palace Avenue.

Some Paignton historians believe that William of Orange or an aide would have addressed the citizens of Paignton to explain why 15,000 soldiers had descended on their town. The base of Paignton's old cross that is now in the grounds of Paignton Parish Church once stood in the centre of the higher part of Church Street. It is on the base of this ancient cross any proclamation or announcement would have been made to the town's people.

On the evening of 6 November, like the previous evening, William and his advisors finalised the plans for the march on 7 November and to their next destination, Newton Abbot.

7 NOVEMBER 1688 – PAIGNTON TO NEWTON ABBOT

At Torre Abbey, the old Premonstratensian monastery that faces the seafront at Torquay, there was rejoicing. Elizabeth Cary (step-mother of Edward Cary the owner of the Abbey) and her priest looked out to sea and saw the white flags fluttering at the top of the masts of the Dutch fleet. 'The French!' they thought. 'The long awaited French Catholics'. But why would they think this? William of Orange had ordered that when sailing into Torbay, white flags should be flown uppermost to signify peace. But Elizabeth Cary mistook these white flags as the symbol of the French Navy. Celebrating, the priest ordered that the 'Te Deum' be sung in the chapel which start with the words 'Thee O God we praise'. Elizabeth Cary and the priest were in for a nasty surprise.

On 7 November 1688 soldiers arrived searching for arms and horses. William had given orders that Roman Catholic homes including Torre Abbey and Ugbrooke House near Chudleigh should be searched. Elizabeth Cary and her priest realised that they were deceived, and everyone fled except her and a few servants. There were rumours that the soldiers set fire to the Abbey, but these rumours were false.

The bulk of the army commenced the march to Newton Abbot and there is an old Dutch map that shows the route William of Orange and his army took when marching from Brixham to Paignton on 6 November and then on to Newton Abbot on 7 November. The route out of Paignton was up today's Marldon Road in a north westerly direction and towards the village of Marldon.

Here the troops would have joined and followed the ancient highway from Kingswear to Newton Abbot described in John Ogilby's map of 1675. However, it was no better than a muddy 21st-century bridleway and, when between hedgerows, the road was no more than four feet wide and the army continued to become stuck in the muddy lanes of Devon. Their route went past Marldon Church, Compton Castle, Compton Mill, and Bickley Mill (now the Bickley Mill Restaurant) to Maddacombe Cross and then on to Abbotskerswell and Newton Bushell, the old name for Newton Abbot.

Constantijn Huygens marched with the troops from Paignton to Newton Abbot, a journey of eight miles. He describes the countryside as having: 'great and high mountains and deep valleys, everything separated by tall hedges… the roads of loose stones and slippery.' In others words, typical South Devon countryside that was completely alien to the Dutch. Women, men and children lined their route and cried out: 'God bless you' and one old woman wanted to serve William with a drink of mead, whilst others, remembering the fate of those supporting the Duke of Monmouth, hid behind the men, fearful of the consequences of fraternising with William and his men.

William Bentinck's 'Order of March' also shows that whilst some troops marched on this Marldon to Abbotskerswell route, some marched via Kingskerswell.

Accompanying William on the first two days of the march were Marshal Schomberg, Count Heinrich Maastricht Solms (William's cousin), Count Nassau, William Bentinck, William Frederick Zuylestein (William's Cousin), the Earl of Shrewsbury, the Earl of Macclesfield, Viscount Mordaunt, Lord Wiltshire, and several other knights and gentlemen.

So which way did William of Orange ride to Newton Abbot from Paignton? There is a third oral history passed on from the early 19th century by the vicar of Kingskerswell, the Rev Aaron Neck, that gives a clue. He wrote in a letter dated 1851, that his grandmother who was born in the reign of Charles II, remembers standing in the churchyard at Kingskerswell and watching William of Orange ride by. William of Orange is also said to have visited Pitt House, a thatched house near to the church.

But what did Rev Aaron Neck's grandmother see when William of Orange rode by the church? She would have seen an unmistakable man riding a white horse, wearing full body armour, and a plume of white ostrich feathers in his helmet. It was surely an amazing sight for the inhabitants of a tiny Devon village.

John Ogilby's 1675 map shows two routes from Compton to Kingskerswell. One is an extremely steep path through fields to the right just before Compton Castle that then leads to various lanes down to Kingskerswell. The other, less steep route, is a right fork after the Compton Cross junction to the hamlet of North Whilborough and then downhill via ancient Churchway Lane to the parish church.

Another route from Paignton to Kingskerswell could have been via Cockington, Gallows Gate, Edginswell and Colstray Farm in Yon Street, Kingskerswell, where legend has it that some soldiers were billeted. It's possible that William of Orange stopped at Compton Castle or Cockington Court for refreshments.

A question sometimes asked is this: 'Did William of Orange ride past the site of today's Prince of Orange pub in Barton, the northern suburb of Torquay?' There is no historical evidence to suggest that he did, but bearing in mind that his army camped at Milber Down Hill Fort on the eastern outskirts of Newton Abbot on the night of 7 November, and William had 15,000 soldiers, it is quite possible that some soldiers travelled via Barton and on its ancient road to Milber Down.

When William of Orange arrived at Newton Abbot on 7 November 1688 it was market day. He himself did not go into the town centre of Newton Abbot, but went straight to Forde House, the home of Sir William Courtenay. However, the first documented declaration about the reasons for William of Orange coming to England was read to the crowds from the base of Newton Abbot's old cross in the town centre. John Whittle gives a detailed account of this declaration and writes that on the march to Newton Abbot: 'a certain divine (one who has authority from God) went before the army and finding that t'was market day he went unto the Cross where pulling out a declaration of the Prince of Orange, with undaunted resolution, began with a loud and audible voice to read as follows':

'William Henry, by the grace of God, Prince of Orange, hereby gives notice of the reasons inducing him to appear in arms in the Kingdom of England, for preserving the Protestant religion, and restoring the Laws and Liberties of England, Scotland and Ireland.'

Figure 10 – St Leonard's Tower and the base of the old cross in Newton Abbot

The base of the old cross dates back to the 13th century and although the cross has long disappeared, the base still exists and is still very near to St

Leonard's Tower. It has an inscription that commemorates the declaration of William of Orange's arrival. The wording is this:

'The first declaration of William III Prince of Orange Glorious Defender of the Protestant religion and the liberties of England were read on this pedestal by the Rev John Reynel Rector of this parish 5 November 1688.'

Unfortunately there are two errors on the inscription stating that the declaration was made on 5 November, and it was read by the vicar of Wolborough, the Rev John Reynel. The date was of course the 7 November, and the declaration was announced by 'the divine' not the vicar of Wolborough. Historians believe that it was John Whittle himself or Dr Gilbert Burnet who read the declaration. And apparently the man who carved the lettering on the pedestal was never paid for his work.

John Whittle then visited Rev John Reynel in his home and asked him for the keys to St Leonard's church so that the bells could be rung. His reply was that he would only hand the keys over if it was a command in the name of William of Orange – which was then given - and the bells were rung this time in honour of William of Orange.

Newton Abbot and the surrounding villages was a safe Protestant town for William to be in. A survey of religion in 1676 shows that in Wolborough, Highweek, Ashburton, Chudleigh and Coffinswell, there were 1,770 conformists and non conformists but only two Papists.

Whittle writes: 'the people of the town were exceedingly cheerful, and began to drink to the Prince of Orange's health'. There were few who were at the market that day who doubted that they were witnessing a revolution. Arguably, 7 November 1688 was the greatest day in Newton Abbot's history.

Whilst the army camped at Milber Down, itself an historic hill fort outside of Newton Abbot, William with the upper echelons of his entourage stayed at Forde House situated on the outskirts of the town.

William of Orange would have ridden down the drive that was, at that time, through the middle of a much larger park and entered through the same front door that exists today. He would have stepped into the Great Hall only to find that 'his host was not at home'. The owner Sir William Courtenay had a political dilemma. King James II was still on the throne and should he not be overthrown, Sir William Courtenay would be considered a traitor for hosting William of Orange. Conversely, if he had not offered hospitality, he would be out of favour with William of Orange if he ever became king.

His wisdom paid off and in 1689 he was rewarded by William of Orange with the title of Baron but never chose to use his title because he was already rightfully the Earl of Devon.

Figure 11 – Forde House in Newton Abbot

William was therefore able to lodge at Forde House on the night of 7 November, and he slept in a room on the 1st floor now called the Orange Room. It's a small room, but he preferred it to the larger King Charles room where his grandfather had slept in 1625 when on his way to inspect the fleet at Plymouth. The Orange Room was secure as it is entered via a servants' room where his guards were stationed. Sometime after his stay the room was painted orange but is now a neutral colour.

William of Orange had followed in the footsteps of others who had stayed at Forde House. As well as Charles I, Sir Thomas Fairfax and his lieutenant Oliver Cromwell stayed at Forde House on their way to capture Dartmouth in 1646 during the Civil War.

8 NOVEMBER 1688 – NEWTON ABBOT TO CHUDLEIGH

On 8 November, William and his army continued their march and headed in the direction of Chudleigh, a journey of seven miles with the intention of marching into Exeter the following day and making the city his headquarters before continuing to London.

Departing from Forde House, William, his entourage and bodyguards rode towards St Leonard's church and up what are now Bank Street,

Highweek Street and Exeter Road. Glancing to his left, William would have seen the 15th-century Highweek church before marching towards and along the old Roman Road that crosses the River Teign.

William rode across the 17th-century, two-arched, limestone Teign Bridge that was replaced in 1815 with the current single span bridge. An archaeological study of its foundations revealed that this route had indeed been used since Roman times and is recognised as a Roman road. The route that William of Orange took is truly ancient and his march added to its historic importance. The approach to the Teign Bridge includes a long causeway which, whilst flat, was probably hard going. Celia Fiennes writes: 'in many places you travel on causeways which are uneven also for want of a continued repair.' One mile on, William passed or entered the Tom the Trumpeter Inn (now the Grade II Sandygate Inn) and a little further on, another inn, called the Red Lion. Both inns are marked on John Ogilby's 1675 map.

Ugbrooke House, situated a short distance from Chudleigh was, and still is, the home of Lord Clifford, who like the Cary family at Torre Abbey was a Roman Catholic. However, there was no resistance at all to the arrival of William of Orange at Chudleigh.

Reaching Chudleigh, William slept one night, according to Mary Jones in her 1875 'The History of Chudleigh', in the Mansion House of the Cholwich family situated in the centre of the town, and he is said to have addressed the inhabitants from one of its windows. Constantijn Huygens wasn't impressed with the town and described it as: 'a little place with very bad houses'.

The bulk of William's army had slept at Milber Down on the night of 7 November and on 8 November many of the soldiers continued their journey to Chudleigh and Exeter by crossing the River Teign estuary via its ancient ford, before spreading out across South Devon to guard the approaches to Exeter. Their 1½-mile march from Milber Down was via Hackney Lane with its final stretch being quite steep where it reaches the Teign estuary.

Once across the river, their march continued up Hackney Lane on the Kingsteignton side. In the distance the soldiers would have spotted Haytor and Rippon Tor high up on Dartmoor, which to them would have looked like mountains. They were no doubt grateful that they did not have to climb them to reach Exeter. However, their march was one long uphill slog to Great Haldon which is over 700 feet above sea level before descending to the valley of the River Exe. William Bentinck's 'Order of March' indicates that some soldiers marched to Exeter from the River Teign estuary via

Kennford, suggesting that these troops were also assessing the strength of any opposition to William in South Devon. There was no resistance and in the words of John Whittle: 'the army moved toward Exeter, some regiments being at one town and some in another'.

William's first four days in England had been a resounding success. It was now the time for the final leg of the march to Exeter.

Meanwhile, Dr Burnet and Lord Mordaunt, accompanied by soldiers, had been sent on ahead from Newton Abbot to Exeter to prepare for his arrival and to find suitable quarters for him. T W Windeatt explains in his Devonshire Association lecture in 1881 that: 'when the advance party arrived at Exeter on the morning of 8 November they found the Westgate closed to them on the orders of the Mayor and Aldermen but without barricading or fastening so that being soon opened, an advance party entered, and was joyfully received by the inhabitants'. An Exeter tradition is that it was Alderman Tuthill who opened the gate.

Lord Mordaunt and Dr Burnet went immediately to the Guildhall and released Captain Hicks who had been imprisoned on the orders of the Mayor for supporting William. He had entered Exeter the day before, declaring for William and: 'great numbers flocked to him to enlist themselves in the Prince's service' much to the concern and annoyance of Mayor Thomas Jefford. Lord Mordaunt and Dr Burnet then requested the mayor to welcome William at the Westgate which he refused because he was under an oath of allegiance to James II. Not surprisingly, he was some time later removed from his position of mayor.

9 NOVEMBER 1688 – CHUDLEIGH TO EXETER

The weather on 9 November was almost continuous rain, and the condition of Devon's roads between Chudleigh and Exeter was as stony and muddy as those already encountered. The first four miles of the ten-mile march from Chudleigh to Exeter followed the Old Exeter Road and was one long uphill climb to reach Great Haldon from where a distant view of the city could be seen. The pragmatic William of Orange might even have been a little excited that the city he would make his headquarters was now within reach. From Great Haldon it was an easier six-mile downhill stretch through the hamlets of Clapham and Shillingford Abbot, the village of Alphington (now a suburb of Exeter) to the walls of the city.

It was during this last stretch of the day's march that the local inhabitants not only expressed their joy at the arrival of William of Orange, but also a desire to fight for him. John Whittle writes:

> 'About five miles off the City, sundry companies of young men met them, with each a club in his hand; and as they approached near, they gave sundry shouts and huzzas, saying, God bless the Prince of Orange, and grant him victory over all his enemies. We are his true servants, and come to fight for him as long as we are able: so we all bid them welcome.'

This display of support must have been heartening for William, but he must have wondered if the gentry would soon show the same enthusiasm and pledge their allegiance to him.

At 1 pm, William entered the Westgate of the city of Exeter with the greatest part of his army. It must have been an amazing sight and is described by John Whittle as being a glorious occasion:

> 'The guards rode, some before and some behind him, with their swords drawn, their colours flying. Kettle drums beating, and trumpets sounding joyfully, their officers courteously bowing unto the people; all sorts and conditions of men thronging on each side of the streets, making great acclamations and huzzas as the Prince passed by. The windows of every house were extremely crowded and beautified; the bells ringing.'

The foot soldiers however, did not appear well, looking very pale and weather-beaten, having marched for four days in the dirt and rain straight after the voyage across the North Sea and down the English Channel. Those who were extremely ill were admitted to the Blue Maid's Hospital in Mary Arches Lane in the city and cared for by John Case and his two servants. A document listing 65 soldiers who were in the hospital is held at the Devon Heritage Centre and it is not surprising that many suffered from fever, swollen legs and 'short breath' having endured the voyage, the march from Brixham in the wet November weather and had slept in the open air. Some were still patients in 1689.

However, by 1706, the city had not been reimbursed for the costs incurred for their care which was: 'Three Hundred Forty Five Pounds Four Shillings and Two Pence halfepenny' being equivalent to around £70,000 in 2022 and reflects the enormous task of caring for so many sick soldiers. Mayor Thomas Barons and the Common Council had the delicate and diplomatic task of writing to Queen Anne to request payment which includes the words: 'we the Mayor, Aldermen and Common Council, of the aforesaid City, humbly beg leave to petition your Gracious Majesty that out of your Majesty's great Justice and Beneficence an Order may be given by your Majesty, for the Reimbursing your Petitioner'. The letter explains that William of Orange promised to: 'reimburse the Chamber such sums as (by them) should be, on this Account expended'. However, it is not known if the account was settled by Queen Anne.

Once inside the city walls, William rode towards the Deanery accompanied, says Whittle, by his senior army officers and advisors: Marshal Schomberg, Count Solms, Count Nassau, Major-General Zuylestein, William Bentinck, the Earl of Shrewsbury, the Earl of Macclesfield, Lord Viscount Mordant, Lord Wiltshire, Earl of Argyle, Colonel Sidney, Sir Rowland Guyn, and several others.

The large crowds pressed forward wanting to catch a glimpse of him, so much so, that he could hardly pass on his horse through the streets. John Whittle describes how one woman, so determined to see William, pushed through the crowds and the Horse Guards shouting, 'I will see him though it cost me my life'. She managed to approach him, touch his hand and then, touching her heart, said in a loud voice, 'Now my very soul within me is the better for seeing him'. Hearing this, William smiled and at that moment in time, he wished for nothing better than those good wishes of the people and he could now at last, make Exeter his temporary headquarters.

Figure 12 – William of Orange entering Exeter (Image – JSTOR digital library)

CHAPTER 8

WILLIAM OF ORANGE IN EXETER

A DESCRIPTION OF EXETER AT THE END OF THE 17th CENTURY

Exeter was the obvious place for William to have his temporary headquarters. It's strategically situated, because every important road in the county of Devon converged on it and it was at the lowest bridging point on the River Exe. It was prosperous and wealthy being the third-largest port outside of London and its main export was woollen cloth. Above all, the city was the ecclesiastical capital of the South West. The city was very secure, being enclosed within its ancient city wall. It had many inns serving the stage-coach traffic, visiting market stall owners and merchants and would have benefited from the custom of the Lords and gentlemen who accompanied William.

Figure 13 – Stepcote Hill, Exeter

Figure 14 – the Bishop's Throne in the Cathedral

William approached Exeter from the west, marched across the medieval and long 13-arched bridge spanning the River Exe, entered the city via the Westgate and may well have ridden his horse up the narrow, cobbled Stepcote Hill towards the Cathedral. This steep hill still exists as a cobbled street enclosed on both sides by terraces of old houses.

Figure 15 – the ruins of the medieval Exe Bridge

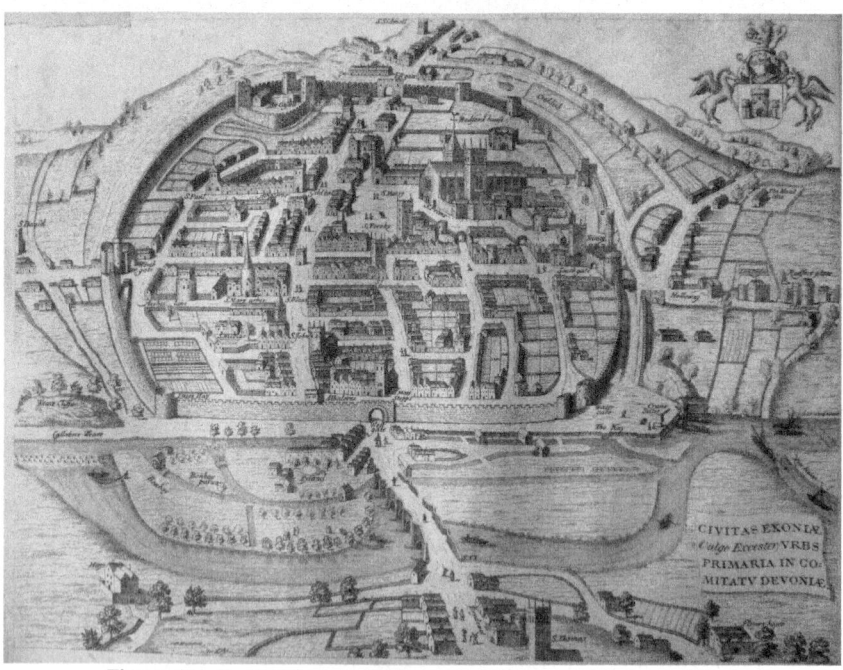

Figure 16 – Exeter circa 1616 (Torquay Museum Society Archive)

Celia Fiennes described Exeter in quite some detail when she visited the city ten years later in 1698. A shortened, paraphrased version follows and the similarities between Exeter then and now are fascinating:

'Exeter is very well built with spacious noble streets. It has a vast serge industry and an incredible quantity is made and sold in the town. A huge number of carriers enter the town with their horses loaded with wool. Friday is market day which is held along many streets and in the large Market House that is set on stone pillars. There is also a square court with penthouses round where the malters sell their malt and oat meal, but the serge is the chief manufacture. The city resembles London, for besides the buildings I mentioned, there is an Exchange full of shops and there is also a very large space railed in just by the Cathedral with walks round it which is called the Exchange for Merchants.

There are seventeen churches in the city and four in the suburbs and there are some remains of the castle walls and the rooms which are inside, are used as the assizes. There is also a Guild Hall, the entrance of which is a large place set on stone pillars, and beyond are the rooms for the session, or meetings about the town's affairs. Behind this building there is a vast cistern replenished from the river which holds about 20,000 gallons of water and supplies by pipes the whole city.

The River Exe has several weirs above the bridge where salmon are caught and several leats have been constructed whose waters power the mills. By the quay is the Custom House and an open space below with rows of pillars in which they lay goods that are unloaded from ships.

The Cathedral at Exeter is a lofty building in the inside with the largest pair of organs I have ever seen and a fine carving of wood which runs up a great height. The Bishop's throne was very high and the carving very fine full of all variety of figures, something like the work over the archbishop's throne in St Paul's, London. There were several good monuments and effigies of Bishops: there was one of a judge and his lady that was very curious.'

The River Exe, the Exe Bridge, the Westgate, Stepcote Hill, the Castle and the Cathedral can all be identified on the 1616 map of Exeter (Figure 16) and some of the Exeter that William of Orange saw and enjoyed still exists today.

9 TO 20 NOVEMBER 1688 - HIS STAY AT EXETER

The events that took place at Exeter between 9 and 20 November 1688 were not as dramatic as those in the English Channel or at Brixham, but were equally important and interesting, because Exeter was the place where William of Orange wanted to consolidate his support and strengthen his army. Exeter was therefore, another significant turning point and milestone in his invasion of England.

There were plenty of problems to address: how many of the local inhabitants should be permitted to join his army, when would the nobility and gentry of Devon swear their allegiance to him, the planning of his march through the rest of Devon and on to London and, would the forces of James II oppose him and where? However, his first priority in Exeter was to thank God for his safe arrival in England.

After refreshing himself in the Deanery, William went to the Cathedral for a service of thanksgiving. He sat in the 15th-century bishop's throne protected by his bodyguards. The organist played and the choir sang the Te Deum, the collects were read and Dr Burnet, sitting on a seat under the pulpit, read the now familiar declaration of William that was first read in Devon at Newton Abbot:

'William Henry, by the grace of God, Prince of Orange, hereby gives notice of the reasons inducing him to appear in arms in the Kingdom of England, for preserving the Protestant religion, and restoring the Laws and Liberties of England, Scotland and Ireland.'

At the beginning of the declaration, the ministers of the Cathedral rushed out of their seats causing a minor commotion and Bishop Lamplough was nowhere to be seen. He had fled to London as soon as he heard that William had landed at Brixham, provided James II with information and was rewarded with the position of the Bishop of York. The Cathedral Dean, Richard Annesley, had already fled into the countryside but did return and Mayor Thomas Jefford, being a Roman Catholic, had declined that invitation to greet William of Orange at the Westgate. So the Cathedral ministers had the same type of dilemma as did Sir William Courtenay of Forde House in Newton Abbot: should one show allegiance to King James II or William of Orange?

The advanced guard of the army marched to Clyst Heath (now a suburb in the south east of Exeter). The heavy artillery that had been shipped to Topsham could now be brought to Exeter, but this was a tough task with some being too heavy for even 16 horses to draw on Devon's atrocious roads. However, bringing the ships up to Topsham and maybe further upstream was not without incident. One ship hit a cliff and there was confusion as to the depth of the River Exe with the rising and falling tides. The majority of the equipment was then taken to Clyst Heath to join the advance guard.

Figure 17 – the Old Deanery in Exeter where William stayed

Figure 18 – Exeter Cathedral in the 18th century

Two days later on the morning of 11 November 1688, Dr Burnet preached in the Cathedral which, says John Whittle was: 'extremely throng'd with people' who had come to see William. Dr Burnet's text was Psalm 107 verse 43: 'Whoso is wise and will observe those things, even they shall understand the loving kindness of the Lord'. He demonstrated God's loving kindness by explaining that the wind in the English Channel had quickly changed from an easterly to a westerly and the fleet was able to sail into Torbay.

Other clergy preached elsewhere because William's clergymen took a lead role in communicating and reinforcing his message that no one had anything to fear if they supported his declaration that: 'The Liberties of England and the Protestant Religion, I will maintain'. For example, Rev Ferguson preached in the Presbyterian Meeting House and his text was from Psalm 94: 'who will rise up for me against evil doers'. The following week on 18 November, John Whittle preached at St Carion's Church. His text was from Isaiah chapter 8: 'neither fear ye their fear, nor be afraid'.

Every day there were crowds waiting outside the Deanery with many travelling 20 miles in the hope of catching a glimpse of William of Orange including the mayor and aldermen of the city who were able to visit him. However, it was three days before any of the Devon gentry appeared before William with the exception of Alderman Tuthill and Mr Burrington of Sampford - most likely Sampford Peverell - who was a Major in the militia. The magistrates and clergy were also backward in declaring for William and this was not only a cause for concern to him, it also dampened his spirit. After all, it was the nobility and gentry that had invited him to England.

His concern soon disappeared when many of the county's gentry did travel to Exeter to meet him. It was said that the Somerset gentry: 'came in briskly with all things useful in abundance, especially with the sinews of war'. Sir Edward Seymour and Dr Burnet decided that a letter of association should be signed by all those declaring for William or else they would be 'as a rope of sand' and 'men might leave us when they pleased'. William agreed and ordered Dr Burnet to draft the letter, which he did. Then, on 15 November this letter was signed by 50 gentry hence pledging their allegiance to William. It clearly stated that they had joined him for the defence of the Protestant religion and being carefully worded, it excluded any reference to a punishment for James II.

Under the instigation of Sir Edward Seymour who was the Recorder of Exeter, the signatories assembled in the Cathedral and presented the letter to William after which he made a speech. It started with an admonishment to them stressing his concern that they were slow in coming over to him: 'we expected you that dwelt so near to our landing would have joined us sooner'. He did however continue with the sentence: 'Therefore gentlemen, friends and fellow-Protestants, we bid you and all your followers a most heartily welcome to our court and camp.' William could now relax a little, and one day, when the weather had improved, he rode around the city and took a look at its castle.

His army and the horses also had a few days rest to regain their strength after the gruelling voyage and march from Brixham, after which John Whittle wrote: 'one man was as good as two when we were at Torbay'. The army was extremely disciplined and an anonymous account attributed to Dr Burnet commends: 'the civil behaviour among them, without Swearing and Damning, and Debauching of Women, as is usual among some Armies, that 'tis an admiration to behold.'

However, additional horses were needed to replace those lost and soldiers were sent north of Exeter for horses. John Whittle writes: 'the country people came daily with their horses to sell and the officers gave great prices for them'. However, horses belonging to Roman Catholics were taken without payment, whilst many of the gentry gladly gave their horses as did the Bishop's son and many others.

Meanwhile, William's soldiers were ordered to keep themselves and their weapons in good order and to ensure they acquired everything needed for the next phase of their march. So many men volunteered to join William's army that the captains could pick and choose their additional soldiers. Plymouth Fort had also declared its allegiance and there were reports that 1,000 tinners from Cornwall had marched to Exeter to join William's army.

William now ordered the army to continue their march in three lines: the first line marched from Exeter as far as Ottery St Mary and was quartered in and near it. The next day the second line marched from Exeter to Ottery St Mary, whilst the first line advanced to Axminster. The third day the last line marched, as before, to Ottery St Mary, the second line advanced to Axminster and the adjacent towns and the first Line advancing to Beaminster and Crewkerne. By this method, William could ensure a safe passage for himself between Exeter and Crewkerne where he would make his new headquarters.

However, on 19 November word came that James II had advanced west and had arrived at Salisbury with 35,000 men and intended to camp on

Salisbury Plain and fight William's army. News also arrived that there had been a skirmish at Wincanton between an advance party of William's forces and soldiers of James II. An important decision was made: it was time to prepare to leave Exeter.

In preparation William had, on 16 November, signed a requisition for the purchase of oxen and wagons to transport baggage and artillery from Exeter to Honiton. He would pay the rate judged as reasonable by the gentry: four shillings per day for four oxen and six shillings a day for six oxen. The requisition also ordered the constable of Kenn and Kennford (villages between Chudleigh and Exeter) to go from house to house in those villages with two soldiers and ordered that the oxen and wagons were to be brought to Exeter on 20 November. However, despite a good price being paid to the farmers, the lack of oxen on the farms would bring practical difficulties to them at the beginning of winter. This requisition is another document held at the 'University of Nottingham Manuscripts and Special Collections': reference number Pw A 2251.

Then, also on 20 November, William received a letter from Admiral Herbert in Torbay with some concerning news. The English fleet was just four miles from his Dutch fleet and Herbert had attempted to leave the bay and confront the English. However, the sea was rough and the wind such that it prevented him doing so and at the same time the wind pushed the English fleet up the English Channel, removing their threat to the Dutch ships. Dr Burnet would have, no doubt, considered the direction and strength of the wind as another act of God's loving kindness.

William's eleven days in Exeter was to come to an end. On 21 November, he departed from the city and marched towards Ottery St Mary and Honiton, knowing that at Exeter he had consolidated his support with the country folk, the city dwellers and the gentry of the county, all declaring for him. His soldiers had been rested and were now spread out across East Devon protecting his path.

He also needed a safe pair of hands to undertake the huge task to guard the city and appointed Sir Edward Seymour as Governor of Exeter.

The letter of appointment to Sir Edward Seymour is held at the Devon Heritage Centre and it explains that William had trust and confidence in him and was: 'assured of his good intentions to support the Protestant religion and the Rights and Liberties of the Kingdom'. Hence William believed that Seymour had the ability to discharge the responsibilities of Governor and have authority over the garrison that remained in Exeter under the command of Colonel Gibson.

CHAPTER 9

FROM EXETER TO HONITON AND AXMINSTER

21 NOVEMBER 1688 – EXETER TO HONITON

On 21 November, William of Orange marched from Exeter to Honiton, a distance of about 18 miles accompanied by many Devon and Somerset gentry. The road to Honiton was broader than those encountered on the journey to Exeter, but it was soft and slippery underfoot, making it difficult for marching, although Celia Fiennes described the Exeter to Honiton road as: 'all gravel...the best road I have met with in the West'. The oxen hired from the farmers in the villages surrounding Exeter pulled some of the artillery and equipment, with the remainder staying in Exeter under the protection of Colonel Gibson's garrison. Constantijn Huygens explains that along the road to Honiton, men, women and children were cheering William and at Honiton none were found who supported James II.

The route out of Exeter was probably via Fore Street, Heavitree which was on the main Exeter to London road. Then, reaching the village of Clyst Honiton, the road followed the course of the Roman Road via Rockbeare, Fairmile and the Fenny Bridge over the River Otter before reaching Honiton.

John Whittle mentioned that William marched from Exeter to Ottery St Mary where he and others lodged for the night in, not surprisingly, crowded houses. Marching to Honiton via Ottery St Mary would have lengthened William's journey. His plan may have been to march first to Ottery St Mary, a journey of 13 miles where he would dine and if there was time, in the darkening winter afternoon, march another seven miles to Honiton which he was able to do. His diversion to Ottery St Mary might have been at Fairmile where William would have marched in a southerly direction and past the 16th-century Cadhay Manor before reaching the town. The most direct route from Ottery St Mary to Honiton was via the hamlet of Alfington to the Fenny Bridge.

Reaching Ottery St Mary and Honiton, William rejoined his advance troops stationed at these two towns. Estimates put the number of troops already stationed at Honiton as being around 1,000 and were under the command of Colonel Tollemache. Celia Fiennes describes Honiton in 1698:

'Here it is they make the fine bone lace in imitation of the Antwerp and Flanders Lace and indeed I think it's as fine, it only will not wash so fine, which

must be the fault in the thread. Honiton is a pretty large place and has a good market house'.

Figure 19 – the site of the Dolphin Inn at Honiton

Figure 20 – the commemoration plaque at Honiton

Being 'a pretty large place' there was at least one inn at Honiton and William lodged in the Dolphin Inn and Huygens slept a few doors from there, in the home of Hugh Baker, a hat seller. The Dolphin Inn still exists in High Street, albeit rebuilt and is now in 2022 an auctioneer's sales room. It also has an external commemoration wall plaque celebrating the visit of William of Orange.

However, there is an intriguing Honiton tradition that William's visit to East Devon in 1688 was not his first. Richard Farquharson in his 1891 'History of Honiton' writes: 'there is a tradition that prior to the revolution of 1688, William, Prince of Orange came to Bovey incognito and received his adherences there, who met in the old quarries of Beer. I think the story is very important as the then owner of Bovey was Major Waldron, MP for Honiton'. Farquharson is referring to Bovey House situated near Beer in East Devon, but he did not mention his source of this historical snippet and it is probably another oral history handed down over the years. Lieutenant-Colonel Edward Waldron being the owner of Bovey House had influence and was second in command in the local militia. Waldron was elected as MP for Honiton in 1685 and 1689 and in 1687, was one who was considered 'doubtful' about the repeal of the Test Act. He was therefore, quite likely to be a supporter of William of Orange. Locally, he was known as 'Major Waldron', a term he apparently enjoyed.

It was at Honiton that Lord Cornbury arrived from Salisbury on 14 November and declared for William. News of this defection reached London the following day where James II's assessment was that the loss was very inconsiderable in itself, but the consequences were exceedingly great. From that moment on, James II did not know who to trust, it demoralised his troops and gave encouragement to the gentry and nobility of other counties to declare for William. Arguably, Honiton was the town that marked the beginning of the end of James II.

22 NOVEMBER 1688 - TO AXMINSTER

At Honiton at 9.30 am on 22 November, the ten-mile march from Honiton to Axminster commenced. It was a miserable journey because it was raining steadily, accompanied by a gale force wind.

From the Dolphin Inn, the route out of Honiton was probably up Chapel Hill, past the old parish church of St Michael and All Angels and then a further steep uphill climb heading towards Mount Pleasant and Wilmington, along today's A35 trunk road. East of Wilmington the route was probably on what are minor roads today, leading to Moorcox Cross, Taunton Cross and Shute Hill Farm.

William was probably unaware that less than half a mile north of Shute Hill Farm was Loughwood Meeting House. It dates from 1653, is one of the oldest of its kind in England and now under the care of the National Trust. It was built in a remote and isolated location for its persecuted Baptist members who believed that the Church of England relied on the corrupt doctrines of Catholicism. They no doubt approved of James II's 1687 'Declaration for Liberty of Conscience' but may well have been a little concerned about how William might treat them if he came to the throne.

Conversely, William might have known about Sir Courtenay Pole, the commander of the local militia who lived one mile south of Shute Hill Farm at Shute Barton, an old manor house dating from 1380. He was related to Sir William Courtenay of Forde House, Newton Abbot. Sir Courtenay Pole had been the Recorder at Honiton and was removed from his post in 1687 because of his objection to the repeal of the Test Act.

From Shute Hill Farm the march to Axminster continued along the Roman Road (now a Byway) that is south of the A35 trunk road. The final section was along Gammon Hill, Yarty Bridge, across the River Axe on today's B3261 minor road and into the town of Axminster.

The people of Axminster might have been waiting for the arrival of William of Orange because they had heard reports of a planned invasion the previous month. The Axminster Ecclesiastica (the church records of the Independent Church at Weycroft on the outskirts of the town), notes that: 'in 1688 about the 8th month, there were great rumours of war and tidings of the nation being invaded by foreigners'. The Duke of Monmouth had in 1685, landed at nearby Lyme Regis, and the people of Axminster may have expected William of Orange to land there too. There was however, great trepidation as to the outcome of any invasion and war by the members of the Independent Church. This too is noted in the Axminster Ecclesiastica: 'great preparations therefore were made for war, and great thoughts of heart in many, what the issue of these rolling providences might be'.

Their memories and experiences of the aftermath of the unsuccessful 1685 invasion of the Duke of Monmouth were still vivid when the Independent Church congregation had to meet in a secret cave from August to November that year to avoid the soldiers of James II searching for the Duke's followers. They were fearful of: 'the bands of rude soldiers ranging up and down in those parts'. It took until October 1686 for the worshippers to feel safe enough to return to their meeting house.

Figure 21 – Loughwood Meeting House

Nearing Axminster, many soldiers had to march for half an hour in knee-high water, whilst others waded up to their thighs across the meandering River Axe and River Yarty. Even after a dry spell of weather, the mud in the surrounding fields was soft underfoot and marching across the flood plains and rivers in fine weather would have been tricky and on a wet, stormy November day it was hazardous and miserable.

Figure 22 – the old Roman road south of the A35 trunk road

Celia Fiennes had described the road between Honiton and Axminster as: 'stony, dirty… and much up and down hills'. William and his army must have been relieved to get to Axminster after a hard march. As at Honiton, there was an advanced guard stationed in the town.

Figure 23 – the River Axe and its flood plain just outside of Axminster

Accompanying William was one who was familiar with East Devon. Three years earlier, John Manley had accompanied the Duke of Monmouth, landed at Lyme Regis and marched to Axminster. Manley avoided capture when Monmouth was defeated and fled to the continent only to return in 1688 with William. Back at Axminster, he successfully recruited in the area and 'borrowed' horses from Sir Courtenay Pole for the onward journey out of Devon and into Somerset.

None of the accounts of the time record where William lodged when in Axminster, but it was quite likely that he stayed in the Dolphin Inn, a large, three-storey posting house on Market Square. It had plenty of stables and plenty of rooms where his trusted advisors could also sleep. The inn eventually became a warehouse and wine vaults which were so badly damaged by fires in 1879 and 1881 that the building was demolished. An alternative hostelry that William could have lodged in was the George Inn, first mentioned in a manorial survey in 1574. Meanwhile, Constantijn Huygens was feeling very disgruntled because he writes: 'I stayed in a bad house, in a room with a bad bed and no chimney'. It must have been miserably cold after being soaked to the skin on the march from Honiton. The thousands of soldiers were camped around the town in tents and were even more cold and miserable. Huygens also records that he was informed by William Bentinck that William or Orange's 'kitchen' had not arrived, and when he was eventually served his bottle of Breda beer, he complained that it tasted salty. Not surprisingly, the march, the weather and the continuing concern about when other notable persons would declare for him were taking their toll on William.

To his relief, it was at Axminster that some 'big guns' declared for him: the Duke of Grafton who was the second illegitimate son of Charles II, Colonel Barkley the escort of Anne, Princess of Denmark (sister to Princess Mary the wife of William of Orange) and most importantly, Lord John Churchill, who later became the 1st Duke of Marlborough. Meanwhile, James II's fears of defections by the gentry and nobility to William had commenced. Churchill was one who the army looked to for leadership and he was a catalyst for the rank and file of James II's army to defect. Knowing this, William ordered William Bentinck to march on to Wincanton with 1,200 horses for those soldiers in James II's army who wished to declare for him and join him.

The Axminster Constable accounts for 1688 and 1689 held at the Devon Heritage Centre might hold a clue as to how long William was in the town. The three constables: John Lidden, William Miller and Richard Harnard carefully recorded the expenditure in those two years and of the 90 entries in the accounts book, the majority relate to payments to William of Orange and his army. For example, Thomas Turner was paid for two horses that would go to Crewkerne with Colonel Luttrell's Regiment. There was a payment of one shilling and six pence for a guide and horse to accompany Lord Cornbury from Axminster to Honiton, thus demonstrating the remoteness of Devon in those times. The most expensive entry in the accounts was for seventeen shillings and six pence for a hogshead of cider (63 gallons) when William was proclaimed king and the people of Axminster were celebrating. John Rood was paid one shilling for straw for the Prince's guard, Margaret Jones was paid five pence for caring for a sick Dutch boy and the doctor was paid three shillings and six pence for caring for a Dutchman lying sick at the Dolphin Inn. The payments for caring for the sick suggest that there was time to engage the services of a doctor in Axminster and hence William was more likely to have been in the town for four days rather than two days, but of course no one can be sure.

What is clear is that his march through Devon was almost at an end because departing from Axminster it was just four miles to the county border and into Somerset. Those miles would be the last four miles of his amazing and incredible 60-mile march through Devon.

CHAPTER 10

THE MARCH INTO SOMERSET AND ON TO LONDON

On either 24 or 26 November 1688, William of Orange and the growing number of men who had joined him marched north out of Axminster along the Fosse Way. The route was on today's A358 road to Chard. At Weycroft just outside the town, William marched over the River Axe where the worshippers at the Independent Chapel felt safe to meet in their church even though: 'the multitudes of soldiers marched along by the public meeting house.' Their fears of persecution were thankfully, unfounded. The army then marched across a stream at Fordwater. Then, four miles from Axminster, the Fosse Way takes a right fork and along the B3167 road. The county border between Devon and Somerset is at this junction and William of Orange had completed his march through Devon

William continued his journey and faced no opposition until he reached Reading. The Battle of Reading occurred on 9 December 1688 where 250 of William's troops, supported by the men of Reading attacked James II's army from an unexpected position. His army fled with 50 dead and there were a few Dutch deaths. James II said that he: 'resolved to withdraw till this violent storm is over'.

William arrived in London on 17 December 1688. Then, five days later on 22 December, James II made an attempt to flee the country, effectively abdicating, but being caught, he was taken back to London. On his return, William ordered him into exile to France.

William was not crowned king or his wife Mary crowned queen until 11 April of the following year. The Glorious Revolution's religious and political victory was also secured during the early months of 1689. Much of the 17th-century's political conflict had been created by the absence of clear guidelines to regulate relations between parliament and the crown, and William and parliament endeavoured to resolve this friction by creating a new framework based on co-operation. This framework became the 1689 Bill of Rights. William had to agree to limiting the powers of a monarch, and increasing that of parliament before he could be crowned king.

The Bill of Rights withdrew the monarch's right to: suspend or implement laws without Parliamentary consent, to raise money without Parliamentary approval, to maintain a standing army without Parliamentary approval, to interfere with the election of MPs or create courts to investigate ecclesiastical issues.

Under this legislation all future monarchs were also required to be communicating Anglicans and this 17th-century legislation still underpins Britain's 21st-century constitution.

It could be argued that in the early decades of the 21st century there is an absence of clear guidelines to regulate relations between Parliament and the position of Prime Minister that, since the end of the Second World War, has slowly but surely taken on an almost presidential-style role. But in 2022, there is not another William of Orange in the Netherlands, who can come to regulate and maintain *'The Liberties of England'*. It is a political problem that Britain will have to resolve itself.

Figure 24 – the Royal Coat of Arms of William III hung in Berry Pomeroy Church

CHAPTER 11

THE LEGACY OF WILLIAM OF ORANGE IN DEVON

Devon in the 21st century is rich in heritage, commemorations and oral history that remember the invasion of William of Orange and his march through the county from 5 November 1688 to 26 November that year.

William of Orange will always be part of Brixham's history. It has its two monuments, an annual parade commemorating his landing and the town has the enduring story of Peter Varwell, the Brixham fisherman who carried William ashore on 5 November 1688.

William held his first parliament at the thatched house now called 'Parliament House' at Longcombe in the parish of Berry Pomeroy. The event is remembered via its commemoration stone. Sir Edward Seymour of nearby Berry Pomeroy Castle became the Governor of Exeter a few weeks later. William may well have slept in Paignton in its old coaching house in Church Street.

Kingskerswell has its oral history about William riding past the parish church on his way to Newton Abbot. And that town can boast that the first declaration about why William had come to England was read from the base of its old cross which was subsequently inscribed with this fact. His army camped at nearby Milber Down Hill Fort.

Sir William Courtenay of Forde House received a letter dated 2 April 1689, signed by the Earl of Shrewsbury, offering him the title of Baron: 'because of the King's immediate favour and opinion of your deserts. It is left to you to choose your own title'. The title acknowledged the hospitality and support provided for William of Orange at Forde House. However, Sir William Courtenay had already been offered a Baronet by Charles I in 1644, but had not taken the title believing that he was rightfully the 5th Earl of Devon. Now, in 1689, he again decided not to use the title of Baron.

Chudleigh too, can remember that William lodged in the town for one night before marching on to Exeter.

It was at Exeter where William gained support from all strata of society: the town and country folk, the gentry, the nobility and a regiment of James II's army. It was the place where he realised that with this growing support his march to London could be a success. An easily missed wall plaque at the bottom of Stepcote Hill in Exeter at the site of the old Westgate remembers that William marched through it, to make Exeter his temporary headquarters.

Figure 25 – the Westgate plaque in Exeter

Honiton was the town where William's advanced guard received Lord Cornbury and his troops, after which James II sensed it was the beginning of the end of his reign. A plaque on an external wall on the site of the old Dolphin Inn commemorates William's stay (Figure 20).

Axminster, being the last Devon town that William lodged in, can be remembered as the place where William's march through Devon was all but over and it was the town where Lord John Churchill joined William and gave the soldiers in the army of James II confidence to change allegiance.

Another Devon link with the invasion of William of Orange is Admiral Arthur Herbert. His exceptional naval skills ensured that the fleet sailed safely down the English Channel and into Torbay. And while the army marched, he continued to guard the South Devon coast, ready to thwart any attack from the navy of James II. He became the MP for Plymouth in December 1688 and for his services to William he was given, in May 1689, the titles of Baron Torbay and the Earl of Torrington. The latter being an abbreviation of the town of Great Torrington in North Devon. Arthur Herbert was married twice but with no children the title of Baron Torbay died with him.

The towns and villages that William of Orange marched from and through in November 1688 will never see anything like it again. Devon will always have a story, a history and an indelible mark unique to England called ' The March of William of Orange through Devon'. It will always be a significant and important part of Devon's history.

REFERENCES

Anon (1688) The Expedition of his Highness the Prince of Orange for England: in Selection from the Harleian Miscellany of Tracts (1793) held in Torquay Museum

Anon (1688) A Further Account of the Prince's Army: in Selection from the Harleian Miscellany of Tracts (1793) held in Torquay Museum

Bainbridge J (2004) Newton Abbot – a History and Celebration of the Town

Burnet Dr G (1724) History of his own time: copy held in Torquay Museum

Brixham Heritage Museum Archives

Chapman G (1998) A History of Axminster to 1910

Devonshire Association Transactions: Couldrey W G (1932) Memories and Antiquities of Paignton, Windeatt E (1886) The Dismissal of Sir Edward Seymour from the Recordership of Totnes by James II, Varwell P (1886) Notes on the Ancient Parish of Brixham, Windeatt T W (1880) The Landing of William of Orange at Brixham, Windeatt T W (1881) William of Orange in Exeter, Yallop H J (1979) Honiton and William, Prince of Orange.

Devon Heritage Centre documents: Axminster Parish Account Book 1688, Letter from W.W. to Sir William Courtenay 1688, Letter from William of Orange to Sir Edward Seymour appointing him as Governor at Exeter, Xerox copies of Exeter City Archive regarding the medical treatment for sick soldiers at the Blue Maid's Hospital, Exeter 1688-1689

Farquharson R A (1891) The History of Honiton Devon compiled from authentic sources

Fiennes C (c1712) Through England on a Side Saddle in the Time of William and Mary: available online

Green E (1892) The March of William of Orange through Somerset

Hoskins W G (1968) Industry, trade and people in Exeter 1688 to 1800

http://www.historyofparliamentonline.org/volume/1660-1690/member/pole-sir-courtenay-1619-95

Howard K W H (1976) (Editor of annotated 1874 publication) The Axminster Ecclesiastica

Jenkins A (1806) The History and Description of the City of Exeter: available online

Johnson D R (1988) William of Orange's Expedition to England 1688

Jones M (1875) The History of Chudleigh

JSTOR digital library: https://www.jstor.org

Lysons Rev D and S (1822) Magna Britannia Volume 6: held in Torquay Museum

Northcote R (1930) Devon - its Moorlands, Stream & Coasts

O'Hagen M (1990) A History of Forde House
Packe J (1984) The Prince it is that's comes
Parnell P (2007) A Paignton Scrapbook
Relation du Voyage d'Angleterre from the Historical Manuscripts Commission 7th Report of 1879: in Johnson D R (1988) William of Orange's Expedition to England 1688
Rhodes A J (1903) Newton Abbot – its history and development
Roberts G (1844) The Life, Progresses and Rebellion of James, Duke of Monmouth
Taylor P T (1821) Discoveries on taking down Tein-Bridge in 'Archaeologia, Volume 19, pages 303-313': available online
Torquay Directory Newspapers held at Torquay Museum Library:
27 December 1848, 3 June 1849, 11 Aug 1880, 31 Oct 1888, 19 July 1899, March 1914,
University of Nottingham Manuscripts and Special Collections learning resource, 'Conflict' at:
https://www.nottingham.ac.uk/manuscriptsandspecialcollections/learning/conflict/introduction.aspx, accessed 9 June 2021
White P (2005) The South-West Highway Atlas for 1675
Whittle Rev J (1669) An Exact Diary of the Late Expedition of His Illustrious Highness the Prince of Orange: available online

INDEX

Act of Uniformity 1662, 7
Aish, 30, 31
Annesley, Richard, 46
Axminster, 1, 7, 49, 53, 54, 55, 56 57
Babbage Juliana, 28
Baron Torbay, 61
Barons, Mayor Thomas, 41
Beaminster, 49
Bentinck, William, 11, 13, 14, 15, 16, 19, 33, 358, 40, 42, 56
Berry Head, 20
Berry Pomeroy, 7, 28, 32, 60
Bill of Rights, 58
Bishop Lamplough, 46
Blue Maid's Hospital, 41
Brill, 14, 15, 18
Brixham, 1, 4, 10, 11, 12, 13, 19, Chapter 6, 29, 31, 33, 34, 41, 45, 46, 49, 60
Brixham Heritage Museum, 23
Burnet, Dr Gilbert, 12, 17, 19, 21, 22, 25, 26, 35, 37, 38, 40, 46, 47, 48, 49, 50
Burrington, Mr, 4
Calais, 18, 21
Captain Clements, 26
Captain Hicks, 40
Cary, Elizabeth, 33
Case, John, 41
Chard, 55
Charles I, 2, 3, 4, 10, 38, 60
Charles II, 4, 5, 6, 7, 35, 56, 60
Cholwich family, 39
Chudleigh, 1, 34, 37, 38, 39, 40, 50, 57, 60
Churchill, Lord John, 56, 61
Churston, 30

Clyst Heath, 51
Clyst Honiton, 49
Colonel, Luttrell, 57
Compton Castle, 34, 35
Compton, Edward, 10
Cornwall, 12, 23, 49
Count Nassau, 17, 35, 42
Count Solms, 17, 22, 42
Courtenay, Sir William, 8, 9, 28, 36, 37, 46, 54, 60
Crewkerne, 49, 56
Cromwell, Oliver, 4, 38
Crowned Rose Tavern, 25
Dartmouth, 12, 13, 14 19, 20, 21, 28, 38
Declaration for Liberty of Conscience, 6, 7, 8, 9, 54
Delph, 14
Dobbins, Thomas, 23
Dolphin Inn, 53, 54, 55, 56, 61
Dort, 14
Dover, 18, 21
Duke of Marlborough, 56
Duke of Monmouth, 13, 14, 28, 34, 53, 54, 55,
Earl of Argyle, 42
Earl of Danby, 10
Earl of Devon, 10, 38, 60
Earl of Macclesfield, 33, 40
Earl of Nottingham, 28, 10, 35, 42, 60
Earl of Torrington, 61
Exeter, 1, 2, 11, 13, 16, 20, 21, 22, 26, 28, 38, 39, 40, 41, 42, Chapter 8, 51, 60, 61,
Exeter Cathedral, 44, 45, 46, 47, 48
Exeter Deanery, 42, 46, 48
Exeter Guild Hall, 45

Exmouth, 13, 20
Fairmile, 51
Fairfax, Sir Thomas, 38
Fiennes, 12, 30, 31, 39, 45, 51, 55
Fishcombe Cove, 25
Five Mile Act 1665, 7
Forde House, 8, 28, 34, 36, 37, 38, 39, 46, 54, 60
Fosse Way, 58
George Inn, 55
Golden Hind, replica of, 27
Goodrington, 31
Gunfleet, 18
Guyn, Sir Rowland, 42
Harlem, 14
Harnard, Richard, 57
Hellevoetsluis, 15, 16
Herbert, Admiral Arthur, 9, 10, 14, 16, 18, 26, 50, 61
HMS Nonsuch, 23
Honiton, 1, 14, 50, 51, 52, 53, 54, 55, 56, 61
Huygens, Constantijn, 12, 16, 17, 18, 24, 25, 29, 31, 33, 34, 39, 51, 53, 56
James II, 1, 3, 4, 5, 6, 7, 8, 9, 10, 12, 14, 15, 17, 18, 26, 32, 37, 40, 46, 48, 49, 50, 51, 54, 56, 58, 60, 61
Jones, Margaret , 57
Kenn, 50
Kennford, 40, 50
King William Cottage, 31
Kingskerswell, 35, 60
Kingswear Castle, 19, 31
Leyden, 14,
Lidden, John, 57
London, 1, 4, 9, 10, 11, 22, 23, 38, 43, 46, 51, 53, 55, 58, 60
Longcombe, 31, 32, 33, 60

Lord Cornbury, 53, 56, 61
Lord Mordaunt, 16, 26, 35, 40
Lord Wiltshire, 35, 42
Loughwood Meeting House, 54
Lyme Regis, 13, 14, 53, 55
Mallock, Rawlyn, 28
Manley, John, 56
Marshal Schomberg, 35, 42
Mary Henrietta Stuart, 2
Mary II, 3, 8, 9, 10, 58,
Mary of Modena, 5, 9
Mary Tudor, 4, 6
Mayor Thomas Jefford, 40, 46
Milber Down, 35, 37, 39, 60
Miller, William, 57
Moretonhampstead, 7
Neck, Rev Aaron, 35
Newton Abbot, 1, 8, 13, 26, 29, 33, 34, 35, 36, 37, 38, 40, 46, 54, 60,
Orange Room, 38
Ottery St Mary, 1, 49, 50, 51
Paignton, 1, 2, 26, 29, 30, 31, 32, 33, 34, 35, 60
Parliament House, 32, 33, 60
Phips, Sir William, 23
Plymouth, 11, 21, 38, 49, 61
Pole, Sir Courtenay, 54, 55,
Portland Bill, 19
Portsmouth, 19, 26
Queen Anne, 41
Reading, 58
Reynel, Rev John, 37
River Dart, 13, 14, 19, 20, 26, 31
River Exe, 26, 40, 43, 45, 46
River Teign, 39, 40
River Thames, 18
Rockbeare, 51
Rood, John, 57
Roope, Nicholas, 28

65

Rotterdam, 14, 16
Russell, Edward, 9, 10
Salisbury, 12, 49, 55
Seymour Sir Edward, 7, 32, 48, 50, 54, 60
Shute Hill Farm, 54
Shute Barton, 53, 54
Somerset, 7, 8, 48, 51, 57, 58,
Southcote, John, 7, 8
Southend-on-Sea, 18
Staverton, 28
Stoke Gabriel, 31
Sidney, Colonel Henry, 10, 14, 42
Taunton, 7, 54
Teignmouth, 20
The Hague, 2, 8, 9, 11, 12
The Immortal 7, 10
The Netherlands, 2, 4, 9, 10, 11, 12, 14, 15, 16, 21, 22, 24, 59
The Test Act, 8, 9, 53, 54
Tollemache, Colonel, 51
Topsham, 26, 46
Torbay, 1, 11, 13, 19, 20, 21, 23, 24, 26, 34, 46, 48, 49, 50, 61
Torre Abbey, 33, 34, 39
Totnes, 7, 8, 11, 13, 26, 28, 29, 30, 31, 32, 54,
Turner, Thomas, 57
Ugbrooke House, 34, 39
United Provinces, 2
Varwell, Peter, 22, 23, 24, 25, 29, 31, 60
Viscount Lumley, 10
Waldron, Edward, 53
Waller, William, 8, 9
Webber, Will, 28
Westgate, 40, 41, 43, 45, 46, 60

Whittle, John, 11, 12, 14, 15, 16, 17, 18, 19, 20, 21, 24, 25, 28, 29, 30, 33, 36, 37, 40, 41, 42, 47, 48, 49, 51
Wilmington, 54
Wincanton, 49, 56
Windeatt, Edward, 26
Windeatt, Samuel, 28
Woolcombe, Robert, 7
Youldon, Mr, 22
Zeeland, 15
Zuylestein, William Frederick, 10, 31, 35, 42

Printed in Great Britain
by Amazon